The Creative Quilter

Techniques & Projects

The Creative Quilter
Techniques & Projects

Pauline Brown

Guild of Master Craftsman Publications Ltd

First published 1999 by
Guild of Master Craftsman Publications Ltd,
166 High Street, Lewes,
East Sussex, BN7 1XU

© Guild of Master Craftsman Publications Ltd 1999

ISBN 1 86108 138 3

Photographs by Zul Mukhida
Cover photography by Zul Mukhida
Illustrations by John Yates

ACKNOWLEDGEMENTS

Many thanks to the makers who lent their work, including Hannelore Braunsberg,
Greta Fitch, Shirley Isaacs, Elspeth Kemp and Margaret Griffiths.
Several companies were generous in supplying materials including:
Whaleys (Bradford) Ltd, Harris Court, Great Horton, Bradford, West Yorkshire
The Contented Cat, The Old Bakery, 27 Church Street, Baldock, Herts
Freudenberg Nonwoven LP, Lowfields Business Park, Elland, West Yorkshire
Kangaroo (suppliers of haberdashery and knitting yarns),
70 High Street, Lewes, East Sussex BN7 1XD

Unless otherwise credited, all the quilting in this book is the work of Pauline Brown.

Designed by Teresa Dearlove
Typeface: Stone serif
Cover design by Ian Smith

Colour origination by Viscan Graphics (Singapore)
Printed by Sun Fung Offset Binding Co. Ltd., China

CONTENTS

INTRODUCTION

Quilting is not just about quilts! This versatile and popular craft can be used to make and decorate all sorts of items. Besides the traditional patchwork or wholecloth quilt, many household items, garments and soft furnishings lend themselves to embellishment with delicate or boldly stitched patterns.

Besides the popular wadded method, there are a number of techniques which use different types of fabric and can stretch your creativity, producing exciting and innovative projects. Although traditionally all quilting was worked entirely by hand, makers now have the opportunity to use the sewing machine, or even combine hand and machine work in the same project.

THE HISTORY OF QUILTING

The origins of quilting in Europe are unclear, although early Greek and Roman sculptures and mosaics often show patterned garments which might have been quilted. Thick felted or padded garments were worn by soldiers as a form of protection. Later, padded jerkins were used to stop soldiers' armour chafing. One of the earliest garments of this type, together with a modern replica, is on show in Canterbury Cathedral, and is said to have been worn by the Black Prince.

There are many examples of quilting in museums dating from the sixteenth century onwards. Silk coverlets and quilted garments, including petticoats, are referred to in inventories of the great houses of the period. The thickness of decorative quilted bedhangings and covers was ideal to keep out draughts in the unheated rooms, whilst linen waistcoats, jackets and caps were often fashioned with quilted designs, which were both ornamental and warm.

With the increased wealth of the eighteenth and nineteenth centuries, more people could afford expensive garments and textiles for their homes. Professional embroiderers and designers were employed by the Court and the landed gentry to create elaborate quilting patterns which emulated the satin stitch and crewel embroidery popular at the time.

At the other end of the social scale, village women, particularly in the north of England and in Wales, developed a tradition of quilting. In and around the Durham area as well as north Yorkshire, Cumbria and the Scottish borders,

Opposite
Elizabeth's Quilt, hand quilted on cotton with a Tudor rose appliqué design and hearts with a cord-and-tassel border

wholecloth quilts with central medallion designs surrounded by borders of plaits, hammocks, cables and twists were popular. The feathers motif is a distinguishing feature of quilts in the north east. Strippy quilts, made of bands of plain fabrics, were stitched with flowing designs running from top to bottom. Often the design was marked on the fabric by a professional or semi-professional quiltmaker, ready for members of quilting clubs, or groups of friends or family to work. They would sit together alongside a large frame, wide enough to take the whole width of the quilt and talk while they worked.

The tradition in rural Wales evolved in a similar way with quilts produced either by professional quilters or by country folk for their own use. In some villages a girl was expected to have at least six quilts for her dowry and special marriage quilts were made to commemorate the happy day. Some might be completed by an itinerant quilter who travelled from farm to farm sometimes carrying her own quilting frame and staying for a month or two until the work was done.

Quilting skills travelled across the Atlantic with the Pilgrim fathers and later immigrants. The pioneering women of those hard times used cast-off clothing to fashion quilts which were the origins of the wonderful tradition of patchwork and quilting which is now widespread in the United States. The Amish people, a strict religious sect centred around Lancaster County, Pennsylvania, are most famous for their quilts in strong, bold design and deep colour combinations. Originally in wool, nowadays they are usually made of plain cotton fabric with large geometric shapes pieced together, on which intricate hand-quilted designs are superimposed.

With the advent of sophisticated manufacturing processes there was a danger that these ancient traditions would be overshadowed by shop-bought coverlets, and to a certain extent this was the case, except in rural districts or poor urban areas. Two World Wars and depression in the twentieth century did little to stop this decline and it was not until the 1970s that quilting in all its forms came to be recognized as a craft worthy of saving from extinction.

QUILTING TODAY

Quilting has come a long way in recent years. Traditional techniques are still used for the skilful production of the many quilts entered for patchwork and quilting shows which are held throughout the country, helping to bring the craft to a wide audience. Whilst these traditions still hold good, there has been a move by textile artists to update techniques and introduce innovative and exciting new ways of making quilts and quilted items. Unusual materials, paints and dyes are used. Original designs are created by people who are seeking to extend quilting methods through their own creative instincts. It is vital that both these areas are encouraged to survive and expand so that the wonderful world of quilting will continue to be enjoyed.

1 EQUIPMENT AND MATERIALS

SEWING EQUIPMENT

One of the advantages of quilting is that you can start with very little equipment; most items will probably already be in your sewing box. A large range of quilting accessories is now available, but apart from a few necessities these can be purchased as and when the need arises. Good craft shops and specialist quilting shops will stock a range of the latest tools and gadgets which are available.

NEEDLES AND PINS

The traditional needles used for hand-quilting are betweens, which are very short with a round eye and sharp point. They come in several sizes from 5 to 12 – the higher the number the finer the needle. Choose the size which suits your method of stitching and one which goes comfortably through the fabric and wadding.

If you are using a thicker embroidery thread or crochet yarn you will need embroidery (or crewel) needles, which have larger eyes and are longer than betweens. For Italian quilting, a large-eyed wool or tapestry needle will be needed for threading the wool.

Pinning the layers of wadding and fabric together is an important aspect of quilting and pins should be fine, long and rust free. Rusty pins will mark the material you are working on. Long, coloured glass-headed pins are also useful as they show up well on large, heavy projects.

SCISSORS AND CUTTING EQUIPMENT

You will need several pairs of scissors – a large pair for cutting out and a smaller pair of embroidery scissors for intricate tasks and for trimming the ends of thread. If you are making your own designs, keep a pair of medium-size or small scissors with sharp points for cutting paper patterns and templates. Paper blunts blades very quickly, so it is advisable to keep your paper scissors apart from the others or mark them with a ribbon tie. Pinking shears, though not essential, will enable you to cut decorative edges.

One of the most useful pieces of equipment which has appeared on the market in recent years is the rotary cutter. This is a small hand-held gadget with replaceable blades which you use in conjunction with a wide quilter's rule and a self-healing cutting mat. Both of these usually have measurements marked on them, so it is a simple task to cut fabrics cleanly and accurately to a specific size. If you are intending to make a number of large quilted or patchwork items, these are worthwhile investments.

THIMBLES

When stitching quilting you will probably find that some protection is necessary for the finger which pushes the needle through the fabric and also for the one underneath. Conventional metal thimbles are readily available, but specialist quilting shops supply the more flexible Japanese-style leather thimbles.

FRAMES

The hoop (or ring) frames normally used for hand quilting are similar to those for embroidery, but deeper. They come in a range of sizes and are either circular or oval. The larger types may be clipped or screwed to a stand. A recent innovation is the tubular clip frame, which makes a rectangle shape and avoids the bias stretch created when mounting work in circular and oval frames. Rectangular artists' stretcher frames are good for small projects. The traditional large quilting frame and stand is similar to the embroiderer's slate or tapestry frame, consisting of two lengths of wood with

webbing attached in between them, with side stretchers, usually held in place with pegs. These are available in sizes up to that suitable for a large quilt.

OTHER SEWING ACCESSORIES

Beeswax is useful for strengthening and preventing the thread from twisting.

A small pair of pliers is invaluable for pulling through the threaded wools when working Italian quilting.

An unpicking tool is also helpful, should you need to adjust your stitching.

SEWING MACHINES

A standard electric zigzag machine with a few basic attachments, such as a walking (or quilting) foot and guide, and a transparent embroidery or appliqué foot, is all that is necessary.

A twin needle and its accompanying foot is useful for stitching parallel lines for Italian quilting and a braiding foot is invaluable for machine couching. If you want to do freestyle quilting, a darning foot will be needed.

Opposite
Sewing equipment

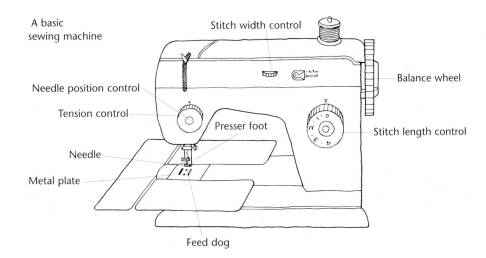

A basic sewing machine

Stitch width control

Balance wheel

Needle position control

Tension control

Presser foot

Stitch length control

Needle

Metal plate

Feed dog

DESIGN EQUIPMENT

Though some people may find the prospect daunting, designing your own project is an exciting idea. In fact, quilting is one of the embroidery techniques which has such a wealth of traditional patterns that it is often a simple matter of arranging these to your satisfaction to fit the shape and size of the item in hand. Although the ability to sketch or draw is an advantage, there are a number of commercially produced accessories which will enable you to create your own designs.

DRAWING EQUIPMENT

Whether you are drawing original designs, adapting printed patterns or simply enlarging or copying projects such as those illustrated in this book, you will need some basic drawing tools and materials.

Large sheets of cartridge paper can be purchased from art shops, along with pencils, felt-tip pens and crayons, all of which will be useful for creating designs. Rulers and geometry instruments such as set squares, compasses and protractors are necessary for drafting geometric designs of squares, circles, triangles and diamonds. Flexible curves will enable you to draw smooth curves.

You may also find graph paper or dressmaker's squared drafting paper useful. Tracing paper can be used for copying, altering or adapting designs, and is essential for making repeat, overlapping or mirrored images.

Design equipment

TEMPLATES AND STENCILS

Templates are shapes which you draw around to create an outline, whilst stencils have slits through which the design is marked. These can be arranged at random, in rows or patterns. Pre-cut templates and stencils are usually made of metal or plastic and come in a variety of designs and shapes, such as hearts and flowers. If you want to design your own, use template plastic which is available from specialist suppliers, or alternatively you can use card or heavy paper. You will need a craft knife and sharp blade to cut out the shapes.

FABRIC MARKERS

Whatever type of marker you choose, it is essential to mark the design lightly, perhaps with a dotted line, which will not show when the stitching is complete. However, some specialist markers are available which will wash out with soap and water, and are therefore useful for items which will eventually be laundered.

The marks made with a blue water-erasable marking pen will disappear when dabbed with water, but care should be taken not to iron the fabric before doing this because heat may set the ink. Test the fabric marker on silk and rayon fabrics to ensure that watermarks are not left when the design is erased.

Air-erasable pens make fine purple marks and stay visible for up to twelve hours, so are only suitable for small short-term projects. Doubts have been expressed regarding the long-term effects both these markers have on fabric fibres, so they should perhaps not be used on items which you intend to be the heirlooms of the future.

Silver and soapstone markers can be sharpened to a point and both wash out with soap and water.

Ordinary HB or B pencils also have their uses, provided the marks are light.

Dressmaker's carbon paper is useful for transferring designs for small projects.

Masking tape is good, not only for taping the fabric and designs to your working surface, but can also be used as a guide when quilting straight lines. It is available from quilting shops in several widths.

THREADS

There is a wide variety of threads on the market, all available in a large range of colours. It is usual, though not essential, to match the thread fibre content to that of the fabric – cotton thread with cotton and silk with silk. Ordinary sewing threads come in various thicknesses. Try out the effect of the stitches before deciding which thread to use. Specialist quilting thread, similar to buttonhole thread, is slightly thicker, giving more visual impact and greater durability.

You can also use crochet cottons and embroidery threads, such as pearl cotton or coton à broder for additional texture. For Italian quilting, a soft, thick quilting wool is the traditional choice, though double chunky knitting wool works well For shadow quilting, which uses coloured wools, quilting wool can be specially dyed or you can use knitting or tapestry wool.

FABRICS

It is important to select the most suitable fabric for a quilting project. If the piece is purely decorative its visual impact will often determine your choice, whereas if you are making quilted clothes and soft furnishings, you will need to consider the fabric's durability and its laundering properties.

Different quilting methods require particular fabrics. In theory most closely woven fabrics are suitable for quilting, though some are more pliable and others reflect the light, which accentuates the stitchery and texture. With wadded quilting in particular, the main effect is created by the play of light upon the fabric, bringing out the patterns made by the stitches. In this instance, a plain light-coloured shiny fabric, such as white satin, would give the most prominence to the texture and pattern, whereas on a dark matt fabric, such as black or navy wool, the effect of the quilting would be negligible.

Shadow quilting requires a transparent fabric, such as voile or organza, which will show off the filling of felt or threaded wools. Stuffed and corded quilting can be effective if a pliable fabric such as jersey is used, as it will stretch over the padded areas, leaving the background smooth and unpuckered.

Fabrics can be categorized by their fibre content:

Cotton, which includes poplin, lawn, voile, piqué and chintz, is the mainstay of much traditional quilting. Patchwork projects are often carried out in cotton as its firmness and washability make it an ideal choice.

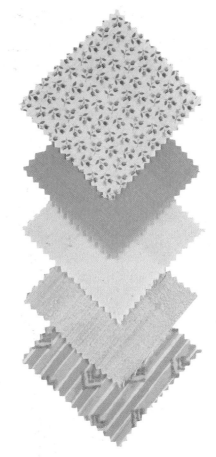

From the top: printed cotton, cotton, calico, silk, furnishing fabric

Silk is a lovely fabric with a natural lustre which shows quilting stitches well. It is available in a range of types and weights from finest honan to heavy silk tweed. Silk organza is suitable for quilting, but silk chiffon, although pliable and giving a lovely effect, is difficult to handle.

Wool was traditionally quilted to provide warmth, but in recent years has lost popularity, although the stretchy qualities of some knitted fabrics makes them a suitable choice for wadded or stuffed quilting projects.

Opposite
A selection
of threads

Man-made fibres, such as polyester, nylon, acrylic or rayon are easily washable and handle well when quilted, though they have a more springy quality than natural fibres.

The selection of either plain or patterned fabric is very much a matter of choice. In general terms, the quilting stitches will show up better on plain fabrics, but for quick and easy projects, printed, painted or stencilled fabrics provide a ready-made design which you can outline, without the need to transfer it to the fabric.

BACKING FABRICS

Different backing fabrics are needed for different sorts of quilting. It is usual to use fabrics of a similar weight and fibre content to that of the top fabric, though on decorative projects, such as quilted panels or hangings, it may be appropriate to use a heavier or different type of fabric. For projects such as quilts, or garments such as waistcoats, which may be reversible, the choice of fabric is important for its effect, whereas for a cushion top, where the underside will not show, plain fabric is acceptable.

Lightweight calicos and cottons are a good choice for most projects.

WADDING

In the past, quilts and quilted garments were padded with anything from scraps of cast-off clothes to pieces of sheep's wool, but nowadays most quilters use a commercially produced wadding.

Besides the fibre content of the wadding the 'loft' or thickness is a consideration, both for the look of the project and its intended use, though it should be remembered that the more dense the quilting, the flatter the wadding will become. In addition, the scale of the project should be worked out and the appropriate loft evaluated.

From the left
fusible fleece, synthetic wadding, cotton wadding, needle-punch, Domette

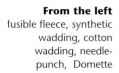

Silk, wool and cotton wadding, the choice of those who wish to keep the fabric content of their projects uniform throughout, is available from specialist shops and handles well. However, it needs careful laundering and gives a fairly flat effect.

Domette is a fluffy knitted type of wadding often used by dressmakers as lightweight padding.

Synthetic polyester wadding is popular and is available in several thicknesses – 2oz and 4oz are the most useful. Practical for the majority of items, it is lightweight, washable and dry-cleanable. It comes in several widths up to that suitable for a king-size quilt.

Needle-punch polyester wadding is dense and firm with little loft, making it a good choice for machine quilting and for small-scale projects.

A recent development is **fusible or iron-on fleece**, which is good for lightly padded items. It eliminates the need for tacking, but its main disadvantage is that the excess bulk in the seams is more tricky to cut away, as it has been fused to the seam allowance.

Nowadays waddings are fire retardant, giving them a slightly stiff feel, which can be eliminated if necessary by rinsing and drying. Although most wadding is white, specialist shops stock a dark grey which is a good choice if you are working with dark fabrics.

JOINING WADDING

Should you need to join the wadding, it can be butted together and stitched with a loosely worked herringbone stitch. For thicker wadding, it may be necessary to work a second row of herringbone on the reverse side.

Joining wadding with herringbone stitch

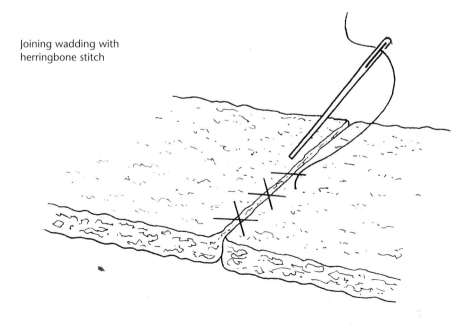

2 PREPARING TO QUILT

The key to successful quilting lies in careful preparation. This includes transferring the design to the fabric, tacking up the layers and framing. Failure to attend to this important stage will nearly always result in a disappointing piece of work with wrinkles and distortions. Unless you are working quick machine quilting, it is usual to mark the design on the top fabric before mounting and framing.

PREPARING THE FABRIC

If the finished quilted piece needs to be washable, use preshrunk fabric or wash it before you start. Most cottons will need to be washed, dried and carefully ironed to ensure that the warp and weft of the fabric lie straight. If you are making a purely decorative piece the fabric will only need pressing.

Always allow at least 2in (5cm) extra fabric around the design to give room for adjustments, framing or mounting.

ENLARGING A DESIGN

For most of the projects in this book simply enlarge the templates on a photocopier by the percentage indicated. If the final size of a design or template is not critical you can experiment by enlarging or reducing until you achieve the desired size.

Large-scale items, which are too big for a photocopier, can be enlarged using the grid system on squared graph or drafting paper. The design contained in each square will need to be enlarged on to a bigger grid, so that all measurements and lines are transposed from the smaller grid to the enlargement grid.

Enlarging a design using a grid

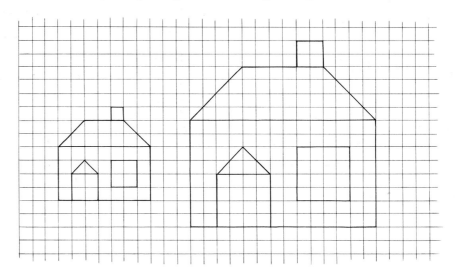

POSITIONING THE DESIGN

The copy or tracing of the design can often be positioned on the fabric by eye. If you need to place the design precisely, for instance in the centre of a piece, you will need to be more accurate.

1   Find the centre of the design by folding it in half horizontally and in half again vertically, and mark the folds with a pencil line.

2   Fold the fabric in a similar way and mark it with two rows of tacking stitches. When you position the design ready for transferring to the fabric the two sets of markings can be aligned.

Positioning the design

TRANSFERRING THE DESIGN

DIRECT TRACING

The simplest method of marking the design on fabric is by direct tracing. Some fabrics, such as fine cotton lawn, polyester cotton, silks and sheer organzas, nylons and voiles, are sufficiently transparent for the design to be placed underneath and traced through the fabric.

Direct tracing

1   Outline the design in black felt-tip pen.

2   Using masking tape, tape the design to your work surface, then tape the fabric in position on top.

3   Trace the design with your chosen fabric marker.

For large-scale projects, start in the centre and work outwards, taking care to keep the fabric in place as you copy over the design.

Tracing and tacking

DRESSMAKER'S CARBON PAPER

Dressmaker's carbon paper is available in several colours – blue, red and white – and is used in a similar way to ordinary carbon paper. Choose a colour which will show up on your fabric. Remember that the marks left by the paper will not wash out, so it is best used on dark fabrics.

1   Tape the fabric to the work surface with masking tape right side up.

2   Tape the traced design in position on top with the dressmaker's carbon paper, coloured side down, between the tracing and the fabric.

3   Using a spent ballpoint pen, draw over the marked lines, pressing firmly. Try not to lean your hand on the tracing as smudges from the carbon paper may result.

Dressmaker's carbon paper

TRACING AND TACKING

Although this technique is not often used for quilting, it is suitable for bold designs and a version of this method can be used for machine quilting (see page 33).

1   Pin the traced design in position on the fabric.

2   Beginning with a secure knot and a backstitch, work small running stitches along the marked lines through both the paper and the fabric. Finish with a double backstitch.

3   Carefully tear away the tracing paper to reveal the tacked line. Remove the tacking as the quilting progresses.

DIRECT TRACING USING A LIGHT BOX OR WINDOW

If the design is not easily visible through the fabric, a light box can be used. This piece of equipment, used by graphic designers, consists of a shallow box topped with glass, containing fluorescent tubes. Although it is an expensive item, it is a good investment if you intend to embark on a number of quilting projects. Just tape the design to the glass surface, then tape the fabric on top and trace through it.

If you do not possess a light box and are working on a fairly small scale the fabric and design can be taped to a lit window.

MASKING TAPE

For a design made up of long straight lines, masking tape can act as a guide line. Available from stationers, art and hardware shops, it comes in several widths. Specialist quilt shops even stock a ¼in (5mm) width.

For slightly curved lines use a narrow tape and, if necessary, snip it along one edge as you place it on the fabric. Simply position the tape on the fabric and stitch alongside it. It can then be removed from most fabrics without harm.

DIRECT DRAWING

Although it is not suitable for the beginner, this method works well with freely drawn large-scale designs, or for geometric patterns drawn with a pair of compasses or a ruler. Secure the fabric which will go on the top of the quilting to your work surface with masking tape and draw the design directly on the fabric using your chosen marker.

STENCILS AND TEMPLATES

Stencils and templates are traditional aids for planning a quilting design. They are particularly useful for creating repeat patterns and often have registration marks or notches at points along the edges to make it easy to position them in the same place each time.

Experienced quilters often use them to mark the design directly on the fabric, but for large-scale or complex designs, which involve the multiple use of templates or stencils, it is usually advisable to plan your design on paper before transferring it. If you are using a single motif, such as a flower in the centre of a cushion, then marking the design directly is a quick and easy option.

STENCILS

Plastic, card and metal stencils can be purchased in a wide range of designs, from traditional hearts, flowers, wreaths and shells to more contemporary motifs. Background designs include simple diamonds, lattice and shells, and borders are available in cables, scrolls, feathers and waves.

Unlike stencils for painted designs, quilting stencils have slits through which just the outline of the design is marked.

Position the stencil and draw through the slits with a fine marker. This produces a broken line which may need to be joined when the stencil is removed.

For a repeat motif, position the stencil carefully by measuring or using the registration marks on the stencil.

TEMPLATES

Templates differ from stencils in that they are usually simple card, plastic or metal shapes, such as circles, hearts, leaves or diamonds, around which you mark. Any lines inside the design are sketched in freehand as the need arises.

Position the template on your paper or fabric and draw around it with your chosen marker. Use the registration marks as for stencils when making repeat designs or overall patterns.

A template

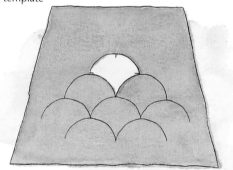

CUTTING YOUR OWN STENCILS AND TEMPLATES

Creating an individual design can be one of the joys of quilting. You can draw your own motif or pattern, or you can trace or photocopy one from printed source material. Concentrate on simple, bold shapes and outlines.

Transparent stencil plastic is available from quilting shops, or you can use card. Plastic is preferable when making stencils, as the slits can be cut accurately with a craft knife and the finished stencil will stand up to extensive use.

Ready-made stencils and templates

1 Using a soft, sharp-pointed pencil, trace the design on to the plastic.

2 Decide where to cut the slits and mark them in a different colour or a fine felt-tip pen. Cut ⅛in (3mm) slits using a craft knife and cutting board.

For templates which are only going to be used as a single motif, or for a particular project, thin card will probably be sufficient. Heavier poster card or plastic is more suitable for templates which will be used frequently.

If you are using transparent plastic, trace the design and cut it out using a craft knife or sharp paper scissors.

If you are using card, cut out the design or tracing and glue it to the card, which can then be cut to shape.

A hand-cut stencil of a sea holly design, sprayed, wadded and machine quilted

FRAMING

Although some people prefer to work quilting in the hand, most projects, unless they are small, can be carried out more successfully if they are mounted in a frame. This will help you to retain the correct stitch tension and the work will remain smooth.

A quilting hoop

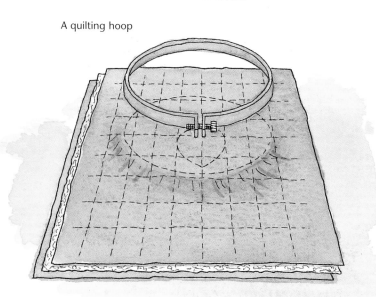

QUILTING HOOPS

These are similar to those used by embroiderers, but they are usually larger and more robust. They consist of a pair of hoops with an adjustable outer ring. They are particularly good for small projects, especially if the whole design will fit within the bounds of the frame. If you need to relocate the frame to another part of the design, make sure that you do not crease or damage previously stitched areas. Remove the work from the frame when you have finished a quilting session, as folds and creases may occur overnight.

1   Adjust the screw of the outer ring so that it fits loosely over the inner ring.

2   Place the tacked fabric and wadding over the inner ring and press the outer ring down over the quilting and the inner ring.

3   Make sure that the grain of the fabric is straight but not unduly taut. Tighten the screw to hold the fabric in place.

TUBULAR CLIP FRAMES

Unlike circular or oval hoops, plastic clip frames have four tubular components make a rectangle, so there is less chance of the quilting being stretched on the bias. The fabric is simply laid over the frame and the outer tubes clamped in place.

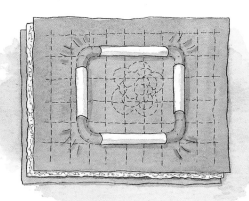

Tubular clip frames

STRETCHER FRAMES

These are suitable for small rectangular items such as panels or pictures, or those on which the design can be confined within the frame. However, do not use them for projects which are already made up or cut to shape prior to quilting, as the pins will damage the fabric.

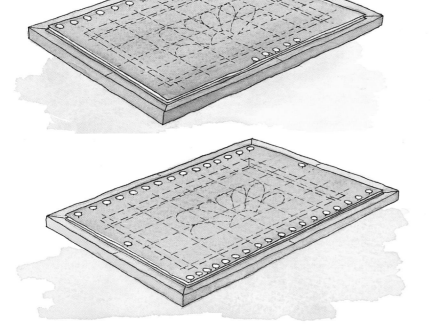

Starting to pin along the sides of the fabric from the centre outwards

Pinning along the lower edge of the stretcher frame

1 Mark the centre of each side of the rectangular frame. Make corresponding marks on the backing fabric.

2 Starting at the top, align the centre marks and secure the fabric with a drawing pin.

3 Continue pinning at 1in (2.5cm) intervals, working towards the corners. Fasten the bottom edge in the same way, stretching the fabric taut.

4 To complete the other two sides, pin the centre points and continue towards the corners, pinning first one side then the other to tension the fabric evenly.

5 Lay the wadding and fabric on top and tack together (see page 21).

QUILTING FRAMES

A traditional full-size quilting frame is too large for today's homes. Tapestry (or slate) frames used by embroiderers are similar, but smaller in scale so are suitable for working sections of garments or small household furnishings. Floor stands are available for the large traditional quilting frames and smaller tapestry frames. When using this type of frame, the backing fabric is framed and the wadding and top fabric tacked on afterwards (see page 21).

1 Mark the centre point of the webbing attached to the rollers, and a corresponding mark at the centre top and bottom of the backing fabric. Pin the top edge of the fabric along the webbing and overcast the two together with strong thread, starting in the centre, working outwards.

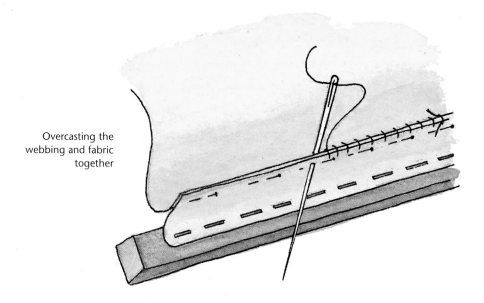

Overcasting the
webbing and fabric
together

2   Roll any excess length of backing fabric on to the bottom roller. Insert the side stretchers and secure them with split pins or pegs, so that the fabric is evenly tensioned, but not too taut.

3   The sides of the fabric are tensioned with pinned lengths of tape. Pin one end of the tape to the edge of the backing fabric. Take it over the side stretcher diagonally and pin again on the edge of the backing. Continue along the length of the stretcher, pulling the tape evenly. Repeat with a second piece of tape along the other edge.

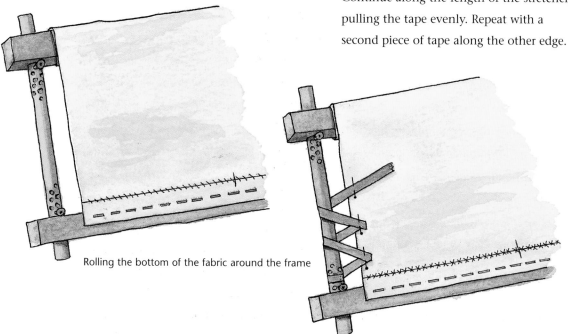

Rolling the bottom of the fabric around the frame

Attaching the tape to the fabric with pins

TACKING

Once the design has been transferred to the fabric the various layers of wadding and fabric need to be tacked together. Do not be tempted to skimp on this, as failure to secure the layers will mean that they will move during the quilting process, leaving the finished piece distorted. Usually, the layers should be tacked together before framing, although in some instances, the backing fabric is framed separately (see below).

PREPARING TO TACK

When working wadded quilting, both by hand and machine, place the marked fabric, right side uppermost, on top of the backing fabric, right side down, with the wadding sandwiched between. Check that the grain lines of the top and backing are aligned.

For Italian, shadow Italian and flat quilting, which involve only two layers of fabric, omit the wadding. For shadow quilting the backing fabric will need to be right side up.

Tacking

1   Pin the layers together with plenty of pins, smoothing out any wrinkles from the centre.

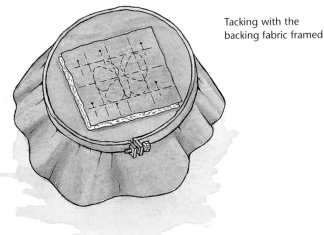

Tacking with the backing fabric framed

2   Starting at the centre, work a row of large tacking stitches, about 2in (5cm) in length, to the lower edge, and then another to the top edge. Then stitch a horizontal row across the centre.

3   Working outwards in a systematic fashion, make rows of tacking stitches about 3in (7cm) apart in a grid formation.

TACKING WITH THE BACKING FABRIC FRAMED

In some instances, such as when using a traditional quilting frame or a tapestry frame, it is preferable to put the backing fabric on the frame before tacking the wadding and top fabric. With decorative padded pictures or panels, where the effect of plenty of loft is required, framing all three tacked-up layers would flatten the wadding. In these cases, frame up the backing fabric. Place the wadding and the top fabric loosely on top. Smooth, pin and tack as above.

Preparation for trapunto quilting (see page 46) can also be done in this way so that when the filling is inserted it stands out in relief on the top fabric.

STARTING TO STITCH

For wadded quilting, particularly on projects which are reversible or where the back needs to look as good as the top layer, it is important to start and finish in as unobtrusive way as possible.

Thread the needle with about 18in (45cm) thread and make a small knot a short distance from the end. Bring the needle up through the three layers to the right side. Tug gently so that the knot pull through the backing fabric and into the wadding. Then commence working your chosen stitch.

For items where the backing fabric is of little importance, or when stitching quilting which only involves two layers of fabric commence stitching either with a double backstitch on the backing fabric or with a small knot.

STITCHING

Whichever stitch you choose, start in the centre of a project and work outwards, smoothing the surface as you go. Work systematically and complete each section before moving on to another. If the design consists of background lines stitch them all in the same direction.

Stitch lines in the same direction

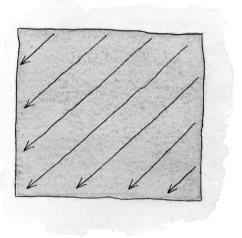

FINISHING

To finish off wadded quilting, take the thread through the wadding a short way. Then bring the needle out through the backing fabric and cut off the thread close to the surface. For other methods, finish with a double backstitch in the backing fabric.

Starting to stitch

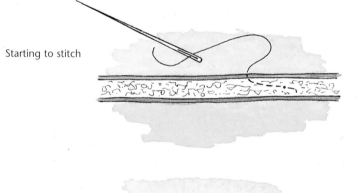

Finishing stitching

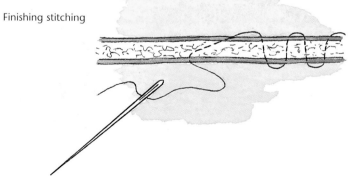

3 STITCHES

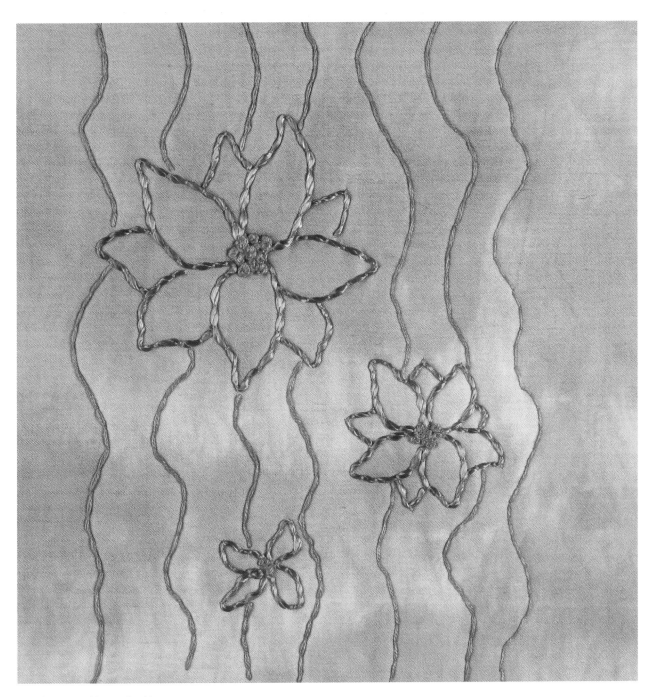

Couching in a shiny embroidery
thread picks up the colour of the
random-dyed cotton fabric

TRADITIONAL STITCHES

The traditional stitches used for quilting are those which produce a continuous or dotted line, such as running, stab or backstitch. They give a clear outline to the design, accommodate the thickness of the wadding and are simple to work. Your choice of stitch will depend not only on the effect you wish to create, but also the method of quilting.

The layers of wadded quilting are usually held together with running or occasionally with stab stitch, although the latter is much slower to complete. Backstitch can also be used, and is very suitable for Italian quilting as it gives a clearly defined outline which holds the cording in place.

Whatever stitch you choose, it is important to achieve a consistent tension and an even length of stitch and, in the case of running stitch, an even distance between each one. This evenness is, in fact, more crucial than the actual size of the stitches. Although you may need a little practice before you can work a perfect row, you will gradually achieve the correct rhythm.

While you are learning the stitches, it is also a good idea to practise using a thimble, usually on the middle finger of the hand on top of the work (usually your dominant hand) and, if you wish, on the first finger of the hand underneath the work.

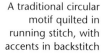

A traditional circular motif quilted in running stitch, with accents in backstitch

RUNNING STITCH

Running stitch makes a broken line. Working from right to left (or left to right if you are lefthanded), bring the needle in and out of the layers of fabric, making small evenly spaced stitches. Depending on the thickness of the wadding, you will probably be able to pick up two or three stitches before pulling the needle through. You can use the hand underneath to guide the needle and push the needle with the thimble on the top hand.

Backstitch

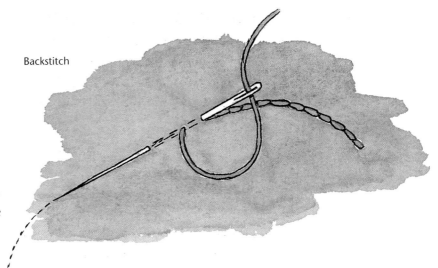

Running stitch

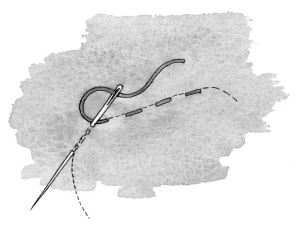

BACKSTITCH

Backstitch gives a continuous line, similar to machine stitching but it does not give a presentable finish on the other side. Bring the needle up a short distance from the starting point, then take a small stitch back through the layers of fabric at the starting point. Bring the needle out ahead of the first stitch and repeat.

STAB STITCH

Stab stitch makes a small dotted line similar to running stitch, but the stitches are worked singly. Bring the needle vertically up through the layers of fabric and take it down again vertically a short distance away. Although this is much slower to work than running stitch, it gives a precise indentation and the individual stitches can be tiny and pulled tight.

Stab stitch

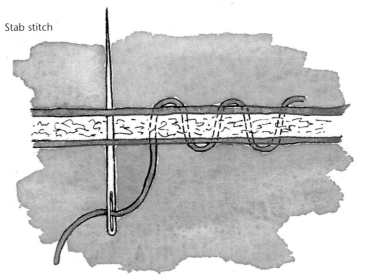

A printed silk, outlined in chain stitch and raised with Italian and trapunto quilting

DECORATIVE STITCHES

Besides the traditional quilting stitches other conventional line stitches, such as stem, chain and couching, can all be used decoratively. If you are making a quilted panel or picture, where the look of the back of the work is of no importance, you can use any type of embroidery stitches. You may need to make some adjustments in the tension and size of the stitches.

STEM STITCH

Stem stitch produces a rope-like line and can be worked decoratively on trapunto and wadded quilting to create an alternative texture or outline.

1   Working from left to right (or right to left if you are lefthanded), bring the needle out on the stitching line, take it down a short distance along again on the stitching line.

2   Keeping the thread loosely above the stitching line, bring the needle up again halfway along the length of the first stitch. Pull the stitch tight and repeat.

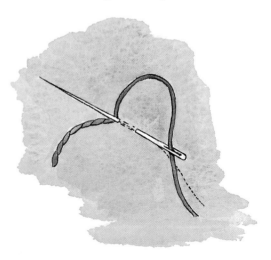

Stem stitch

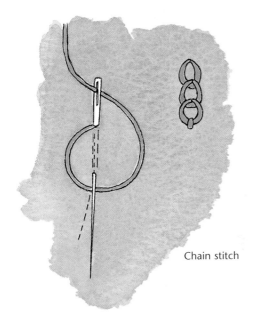

Chain stitch

CHAIN STITCH

Chain stitch is an effective stitch which makes a slightly raised line of continuous loops.

1 Work towards yourself from top to bottom. Bring the needle out on the stitching line and insert it again in the same hole, leaving a loop.

2 Bring the needle up through the loop below the starting point and repeat.

3 To finish, take a small vertical stitch over the bottom of the loop.

COUCHING

Although this is not a traditional quilting stitch, couching is quick to do and gives a decorative effect for designs which require clearly defined lines of stitchery. Threads are laid on the surface of the fabric and secured by means of a series of small stitches at regular intervals in a second thread. It is a useful stitch because it allows heavy decorative threads, which may be too thick to be stitched through the wadding, to be used. Couching is best worked with the fabric mounted in a frame.

1 Bring out the thread which is going to be couched at the start of the stitching line. Thread up a second thread, suitable to be sewn into the quilting, and bring it up a short distance along the stitching line.

2 Hold the couched thread taut with your non-working hand and take a small vertical stitch over it with the second thread.

3 Continue to the end of the stitching line and fasten off. Take the couched thread through to the back of the work and fasten off.

Couching

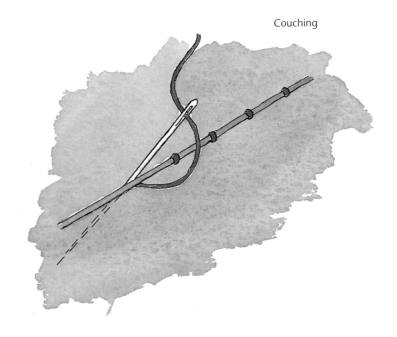

4 FINISHING
TECHNIQUES

A small patchwork quilted hanging is complemented with a bound edge

A neatly worked binding, piping or cord can add a professional finish to your work. A simple article can be enhanced with well-chosen additions, whilst a good piece of work could be ruined with badly made or unsympathetic finishings. Your choice of trimming will depend on the quilting technique used and the effect you wish to create.

Quilts, place mats and reversible items in wadded quilting lend themselves to being bound, in the same fabric or a contrast.

Piping or cords are suitable for cushions, bags or other projects which are seamed.

Choose fabrics or threads which harmonize or contrast with the main fabric of the piece and consider the scale of the finish in relation to that of the whole. Purchased bindings and cords are another option, but those made specially will add that extra touch of class.

Binding

Usually binding consists of a bias strip cut diagonally across the grain of the fabric. The binding strip will need to be twice as wide as the seam or edge it is going to cover, with an extra ½in (1.5cm) so that the raw edges of the binding can be tucked under at each side.

Lengths of bias strip can be joined together on the straight grain to make a longer strip.

Attaching binding

1   With the right sides together, align the raw edges of the binding and the article. Pin, tack and stitch along the stitching line. Clip the curves into any inward corners. Allow extra binding to go around outside corners.

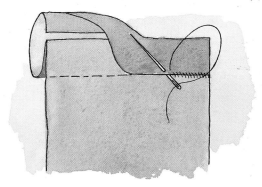

Attaching a bias strip

2   Fold the binding in half lengthwise, turn under the raw edge and slip stitch it to the stitching on the wrong side of the work.

Joining bias

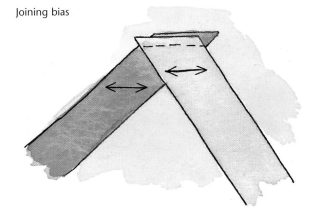

PIPING

Piping is a finish which is inserted in a seam as a raised fabric-covered cord. Piping cord is available in several thicknesses and although some types are pre-shrunk, it is advisable to wash it in boiling water and dry before use just in case.

Joining piping

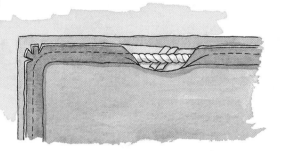

1   Cut and, if necessary, join a bias strip twice the width of the piping cord, plus twice the seam allowance.

2   With right side out, fold the bias strip over the piping cord with the raw edges together. Tack and machine stitch with a piping or zipper foot attached to your machine to hold. Leave the ends unstitched for joining later.

3   With raw edges aligned, pin, tack and machine stitch the piping to the right side of the article, clipping curves and corners.

The simplest way to join piping is to butt the ends together, fold over the bias strip and stitch it in place.

TWISTED CORDS

Handmade cords can be stitched to cover a seam, used as decorative fastenings or as couched embroidery threads.

To estimate the thickness and length of yarn needed, experiment by twisting a few strands together. You will need about three times the finished length.

1   Ask someone to hold one end of a group of threads (or attach to a door knob) and, keeping them taut, twist the threads tightly until they curl back on themselves.

2   Bring the two ends together and fold the length in half, so that the threads twist together to form the cord.

Twisting a cord

5 QUILTING TECHNIQUES

A repeating scroll
motif in stab stitch

WADDED QUILTING

Wadded quilting, also known as English quilting, is probably the most popular of all quilting techniques. It is the method traditionally used for Durham, Welsh and patchwork quilts of all types. Three layers – fabric, wadding and backing – are tacked and stitched with decorative patterns.

This type of quilting is suitable for a large number of projects: soft furnishings of all types, garments and padded accessories such as bags. One of its advantages is that, by using different fabrics for the front and back, it can be made completely reversible, so it is an ideal technique for making items such as quilts, table mats and waistcoats.

If the back of the quilting will not be seen, such as with a lined garment or on the inside of a cushion, choose a plain backing fabric similar in weight to the top.

Hand-marbled fabric with outlines of back and running stitch in toning threads. Some areas are flattened with small seeding stitches

QUILTING ON PLAIN FABRIC

The choice of fabric and thread, together with the quilting patterns, contributes to the design. If quilting is carried out with threads of a similar colour to the plain background, the effect will rely on the play of light on the raised areas created by the stitches. Light-coloured shiny silks or satins will show up the design more clearly than matt dark fabrics. If the quilting design is intricate, using a contrasting thread will define it more clearly.

QUILTING ON PATTERNED FABRIC

One of the advantages of quilting patterned fabric, or those with a hand-painted, stencilled or printed design, is that there is no need to mark the design,

just stitch around the outline of the motifs or patterns featured in the fabric design. Additional quilting stitches may be needed to flatten the background. Tiny seeding stitches worked randomly over a background achieve this successfully.

If an all-over small print fabric is to be quilted with a design which disregards the pattern, the effect of the stitching will be negligible, unless a heavy thread is used.

MATERIALS

Top fabric Plain or patterned lightweight cotton, poplin, lawn, piqué, calico, glazed cotton; silk dupion, twill, honan and shantung; fine woollens; polyester and man-made fibres

Wadding Synthetic wadding, silk, cotton or wool wadding, suitable in weight for the size and use of the project

Backing As for the top fabric

THREADS

Quilting thread, sewing cotton, crochet cotton, embroidery cottons and silks

NEEDLES

Betweens or an embroidery needle

1   Mark the design on the top fabric using stencils, templates, masking tape, dressmaker's carbon paper, tracing and tacking or direct tracing.

2   Tack up the three layers in a grid pattern.

3   Attach the work to a frame (unless it is a small piece or is cut to finished shape).

4   Stitch using running stitch, backstitch, stab stitch or a decorative embroidery stitch.

MACHINE METHOD

Wadded quilting by machine can be worked in a similar way to the hand method. A quilting guide, which is attached to the presser bar, is useful when stitching parallel lines in straight, diamond and grid patterns. A walking foot will ride

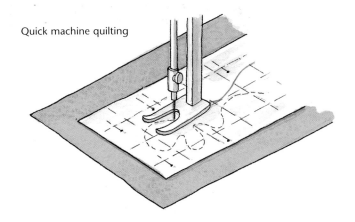

Quick machine quilting

over the thickness of the wadding; if using a regular sewing foot, you may need to ease the fabric slightly beneath the needle.

EQUIPMENT

Foot Regular foot, walking foot, transparent appliqué foot, or open embroidery foot

Needle Size 90–100

QUICK MACHINE METHOD

1   Tack up the three layers – top fabric, wadding and backing fabric – in a grid pattern as for hand-stitched wadded quilting.

2   Transfer the design to tracing or greaseproof paper.

3   Pin and tack the paper design on top of the prepared fabrics through all the layers.

4   Set a long stitch and machine through the layers, following the lines marked on the paper.

5   Carefully tear away the paper to reveal the stitching. Thread the loose ends on a needle, take them to the back of the work and fasten off.

Wadded quilting for patchwork

The traditional way to pad most types of patchwork is by using wadded quilting. American blocks, log cabin, Dresden plate and many other patterns all lend themselves to being enhanced with quilting, which not only serves to hold the wadding and backing in place, but also adds another decorative dimension.

If the quilting is to play a secondary part in the design and is only being used to keep the layers together, the most usual way is to quilt 'in the ditch', with small running stitches worked along the seam lines, making them almost invisible.

An alternative is contour quilting, consisting of a line of running stitches echoing the outlines of the patchwork design. These are usually worked about ¼in (5mm) outside or alongside the pieced motif. Further rows of parallel lines can be added, making a contoured design and an additional row is sometimes worked on the inside of the motif. Both these methods of stitching have the advantage that there is no need to mark the design on the fabric.

For patchwork projects in plain fabric or those which use a combination of plain and patterned fabrics, there is more scope for including intricate quilted designs on the plain areas, such as those normally associated with wadded quilting.

Machine method

As with hand quilting, patchwork lends itself to being quilted by machine, either in the seam, as contour quilting, or across the pieced pattern. Large patchwork projects, such as quilts, need to be handled with care so as not to distort the shape, especially when stitching across the bias, which may stretch.

Equipment

Foot Regular foot, walking foot, transparent appliqué foot or open embroidery foot

Needle

Needle size 90-100

Designs

If the object of quilting an article is simply to create a padded effect and to hold the layers of fabric and wadding together, all-over patterns using stripes, checks or diamonds are the most obvious option. These can be created using a ruler and fabric marker and can be marked directly on to the fabric.

For large projects it is advisable to work out the design on paper before transferring it to the fabric, but simple motifs or borders can be marked on the fabric immediately.

If you wish to create your own designs, use simple bold motifs and patterns with space between the lines. Draw out the design and take a tracing ready for transferring to the fabric.

Spanish Garden Quilt, 96 x 129in (244 x 320cm) by Greta Fitchett, machine-pieced dress cottons with hand quilting across the seams

PILLOW QUILTING

Cotton fabric pillows are joined with zigzag machine stitching

Pillow, or cushion quilting, consists of individually made padded pillows, which are then oversewn or stitched together with decorative stitches such as herringbone or faggoting. They can also be sewn together by machine using a wide zigzag stitch.

The pillows can be made in any straight-sided geometric shape – squares, rectangles, triangles, hexagons or diamonds. With care the entire piece can be made reversible.

The construction of the pillows creates a padded effect, but can be further enhanced with stitches if desired. This technique is suitable for wallhangings, quilts, cushions and simple garments.

MATERIALS

Top fabric Plain or patterned lightweight cotton, poplin, lawn, piqué, calico, glazed cotton; silk dupion, twill, honan and shantung; fine woollens; polyester and man-made mixtures
Wadding Synthetic wadding, silk, cotton or wool wadding, suitable in weight for the size and use of the project
Backing As for the top fabric

THREADS

Quilting thread, sewing cotton, crochet cotton, embroidery cottons and silks

NEEDLES

Betweens or an embroidery needle

1   Cut out two identical geometric pieces of fabric for each pillow, together with a similarly shaped piece of wadding.

2   Assemble the front and back pieces with their right sides together and place the wadding on top. Tack and stitch around the edges, leaving a gap so the work can be turned to the right side. Trim away the excess wadding from the seam and snip the fabric at the corners.

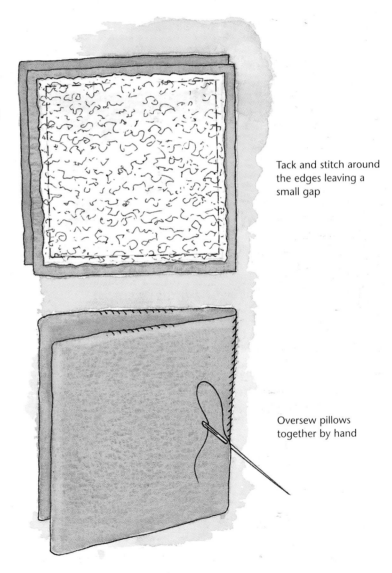

Tack and stitch around the edges leaving a small gap

Oversew pillows together by hand

3   Turn through to the right side and stitch up the gap by oversewing. Press the seam lightly.

4   Stitch together the various pillows by oversewing. Alternatively use herringbone or faggoting stitch.

5   Quilt using running stitch, backstitch, stab stitch or a decorative embroidery stitch (see page 24–27).

EQUIPMENT
Foot Regular foot
Needle Size 90–100

Link pillows with zigzag machine quilting

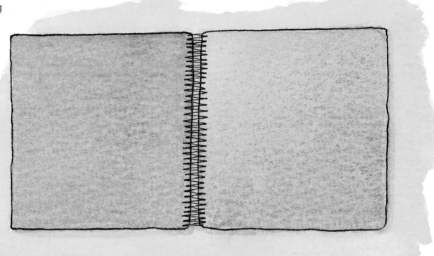

MACHINE METHOD

Pillow quilting can be stitched almost entirely by machine, making it an ideal technique for large wallhangings or throws. The individual pillows are machine stitched around the edges and the gaps are closed by oversewing by hand. Set the machine to its widest zigzag, butt the edges of two adjacent pillows together and stitch so that the swing needle pierces alternate edges.

DESIGNS

This method has the effect of padded patchwork, so most geometric patchwork patterns can be adapted to it effectively. Hexagons will combine successfully with triangles and diamonds; squares with rectangles or octagons. Work out the design on squared or isometric paper and cut out templates for each section, adding seam allowances to each side.

QUILT-AS-YOU-GO

Diagonal quilt-as-you-go strips in plain and patterned shades of blue

Like pillow quilting, quilt-as-you-go combines patchwork and quilting in one operation. Quilt-as-you go is usually machine stitched, although you can also stitch by hand. The technique is simple – random or similar width strips of fabric are stitched to a base of wadding and backing fabric. Designs are restricted to stripes or combinations of stripes. If working diagonally, start in the centre of the wadding and work outwards.

MATERIALS

Top fabric Plain or patterned cotton, poplin, lawn, piqué, calico, glazed cotton; silk dupion, twill, honan and shantung; fine woollens; polyester and man-made fibres; also thicker fabrics such as furnishing fabrics, velvet and corduroy

Wadding Synthetic wadding, suitable in weight for the size and use of the project

Backing Plain cotton if the back is not to be visible, otherwise a fabric which complements the top layer

THREADS
Sewing cotton or polyester thread

NEEDLES
Embroidery needle, if stitching by hand

1 Tack up the wadding to the backing fabric with a grid pattern.

2 Pin and tack the first strip, right side up, along one edge of the wadding and backing with the raw edges aligned.

3 Place the second strip on top of the first so that the right sides are together and stitch through all the layers along the inner edge.

4 Fold the second strip so that the right side is uppermost and continue adding further strips in the same way.

5 Sew the edges of the first and last strips in place.

MACHINE METHOD
The machine method for quilt-as-you-go is worked in a similar way to the hand method.

EQUIPMENT
Foot Regular foot or walking foot
Needle Size 90–100

DESIGNS
One of the advantages of this type of quilting is that different types and weights of fabric can be used for the same project. It is useful for cushions and quilts, or for those articles on which the back does not need additional lining, such as table mats or waistcoats. Large items such as quilts can be constructed by making a series of blocks which are seamed together and finished with an additional lining. The edges of small-scale projects such as place mats or bags can be finished with binding. Cushion tops can be piped.

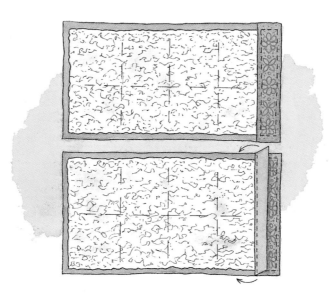

Sew the first strip in place, right side up

Place the second strip right sides together with the first

TIED QUILTING

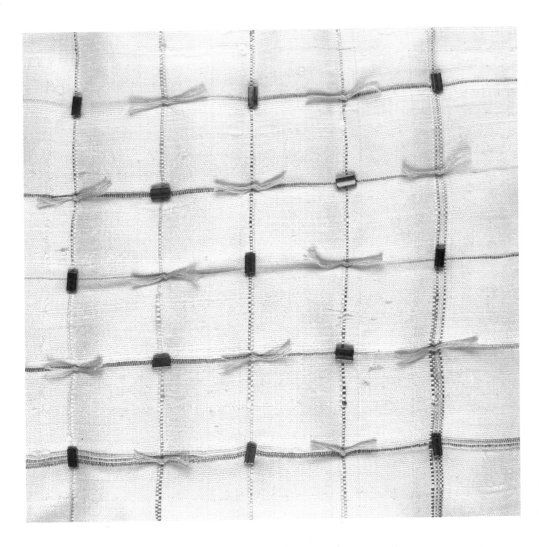

Silk with a woven
check design is tied
with conventional ties
and glass beads

Tied quilting is a variation of wadded quilting which uses three layers: top fabric, wadding and backing. Tying is one of the quickest ways of securing the layers together and can be used for patchwork quilts, cushions and other soft furnishings. The tied stitches, placed at intervals, can be worked almost invisibly creating indentations in the surface of the fabric, or more decoratively with contrasting threads, tassels, beads, sequins or buttons. A variation would be to work small blocks of satin stitch or freestyle stitching on the sewing machine. Almost any fabric is suitable.

MATERIALS

Top fabric Plain or patterned lightweight cotton, poplin, lawn, piqué, calico, glazed cotton; silk dupion, twill, honan and shantung; fine woollens; polyester and man-made mixtures; also thicker fabrics such as furnishing fabrics, velvet and corduroy; patchwork

Wadding Synthetic wadding, suitable in weight for the size and use of the project

Backing As for the top fabric, plain cotton if the back is not to be visible, otherwise a fabric which complements the top

THREADS

Crochet cotton, pearl cotton, coton à broder, decorative embroidery threads

NEEDLES

Large-eyed embroidery needle

1   Mark the design on the top fabric.

2   Tack up the three layers in a grid pattern.

3   To make the ties, start at the centre and gradually work outwards. Work a double backstitch through all the layers, leaving both ends loose. Tie the ends in a reef knot, either on the top surface or underneath. Snip the ends to the required length.

4   If using a decorative, soft thread the ends can be fluffed out to form a tassel.

5   Alternatively stitch beads, buttons, or sequins firmly through all layers.

MACHINE METHOD

A variation on tied quilting can be made by replacing the ties with small blocks of machine satin stitch, worked by setting the stitch width to its widest, and the stitch length to very short. Alternatively small patterns, such as circles or flowers, in freely worked machine stitches can be made.

EQUIPMENT

Foot Regular foot, darning foot for free machining
Needle Size 90–100

DESIGNS

If you are tying a patchwork project, there is no need to mark the positions of the ties on the fabric. Simply choose the positions with regard to the motifs or the pattern, making a regularly spaced design of ties.

If the fabric is plain, and you intend the ties to form a design, work out the placement on paper and transfer it to the top fabric by measuring or tracing.

Depending on the scale of the project, ties can be anything from 1in (2.5cm) to 10in (25cm) apart. They can be placed in grid formation or in a random fashion to form shapes and curves on the surface of the quilted fabric, giving a wonderful three-dimensional effect.

FLAT QUILTING

Flat quilting consists of two layers of fabric, a thick top fabric and backing fabric, held together with all-over stitching, giving a slightly raised effect without too much bulk. It can be used to add thickness to lightweight fabrics, or to give areas such as cuffs or collars protection against hard wear.

As there is no padding, the effect is created by lines of stitches. Emphasize these by using a thick embroidery thread such as pearl cotton or crochet cotton (see also Sashiko and Kantha quilting, pages 44–45).

MATERIALS

Top fabric Medium and heavyweight plain cotton, calico; silk dupion, tweed, twill and shantung; woollens and jerseys, medium and heavyweight man-made fibres; felt
Backing Lightweight plain cotton

The appliqué leaf design is contour quilted through two layers of felt

THREADS

Quilting thread, crochet cotton, embroidery cottons and silks

NEEDLES

Betweens or an embroidery needle

1   Mark the design on the top fabric using stencils, templates, masking tape, dressmaker's carbon paper, tracing and tacking or direct tracing.

2   Tack up the two layers in a grid.

3   Frame up the work (unless it is a small piece or is cut to its finished shape).

4   Stitch in running or stab stitch.

DESIGNS

The stitching for flat quilting needs to be fairly closely made so that the surface is almost completely covered with no large areas left unstitched. Designs similar to those used in wadded quilting can be quilted successfully. All-over patterns are suitable and motifs need to be surrounded by lines or repeat background stitches.

SASHIKO QUILTING

Basketweave and waves are juxtaposed with floral motifs for a typical Sashiko design

Sashiko quilting is a type of flat quilting originally favoured by the Japanese for protective working garments worn by fishermen and firemen. It is traditionally worked on two layers of dark blue indigo-dyed heavy cotton, though any dark colour will effectively show the pattern of running stitches. Soft furnishings and table linen are suitable items for this type of quilting, as are garments and accessories.

MATERIALS
Top fabric Medium and heavyweight plain cotton, calico
Backing Medium and heavyweight plain cotton

THREADS
Crochet cotton, soft embroidery cotton, pearl cotton

NEEDLES
Embroidery needle

1　Mark the design on the top fabric using stencils, templates, dressmaker's carbon paper, or direct tracing.

2　Tack up the two layers in a grid pattern.

3　Frame up the work (unless it is a small piece or is cut to its finished shape).

4　Stitch in running stitch.

DESIGNS
Sashiko is characterized by combining different Japanese patterns such as basket weave, scallops, trellis and waves, with motifs such as butterflies, hemp leaves or persimmon flowers. For a contemporary approach use all-over repeat patterns in strongly contrasting fabric and thread.

KANTHA QUILTING

Traditional Kantha motifs stand out against a background of small quilting stitches

Kantha quilting is a traditional craft from Bangladesh, where women utilize waste materials, such as old saris, to make useful and attractive items like wrapping cloths, coverlets and bags. These are decorated with densely embroidered designs in running stitch depicting symbols and narrative pictures or simply patterns.

MATERIALS
Top fabric Medium and heavyweight plain cotton, calico
Backing Medium and heavyweight plain cotton

THREADS
Stranded cotton

NEEDLES
Embroidery needle

1 Mark the main motifs of the design on the top fabric using stencils, templates, dressmaker's carbon paper, or direct tracing.

2 Tack up the two layers in a grid.

3 Frame up the work (unless it is a small piece or is cut to its finished shape).

4 Stitch in running stitch.

DESIGNS
The effect of Kantha quilting is created by the main motifs, darned in running stitch, set against a background covered with small stitches which give a rippled surface. Typical designs include birds, animals, flowers and leaves, together with geometric patterns, all of which are created with long or short running stitches.

TRAPUNTO QUILTING

The circular shapes of the grapes make this design an ideal candidate for this stuffed method

Also known as stuffed quilting, trapunto quilting relies for its effect on small padded areas which stand out in relief against a flat background. Two layers of fabric are tacked together, the motifs are enclosed with stitches and then stuffed from the reverse side. This method can readily be combined with other types of quilting such as Italian and flat quilting for pictures and wallhangings, cushions and quilts. It is only suitable for articles where the back does not show, such as a cushion top, or an item which is lined. Choose a slightly pliable fabric which will accommodate the stuffing.

MATERIALS

Top fabric Plain lightweight cotton, lawn, fine calico; silk dupion, twill, and shantung; fine woollens and jerseys

Wadding Small scraps of synthetic wadding

Backing Lightweight cotton, lawn or fine calico

NEEDLES
Betweens or embroidery needles, bodkin

1 Mark the design on the top fabric using stencils, templates, dressmaker's carbon paper, or direct tracing.

2 Tack up the two layers in a grid pattern.

3 Frame up the work by inserting the backing into the frame, leaving the top fabric hanging loose.

Stitch along the lines of the design

4 Enclose the areas which are going to be stuffed with backstitch, running stitch or a decorative stitch.

5 Slightly loosen the tension of the fabric in the frame. From the back, cut a small diagonal slit across the centre of the area which is going to be stuffed, making sure that you do not cut through the top fabric.

6 Tease out some small pieces of wadding and gently insert them through the slit using

Gently insert small pieces of wadding through the slit

a blunt instrument such as a bodkin. Check the front of the quilting to make sure the surface is smooth and rounded.

7 Oversew the edges of the slit together.

MACHINE METHOD
The machine method for trapunto quilting is worked in a similar way to the hand method.

EQUIPMENT
Foot Regular foot or walking foot
Needle Size 90–100

DESIGNS
Many of the designs used for wadded quilting are suitable for trapunto, provided the motifs can be enclosed with stitching. Hearts, flower petals, leaves and other rounded shapes are all suitable. Backstitch will give a more defined line than running stitch, so that motifs will show up more clearly in relief.

ITALIAN QUILTING

The curling forms of this leaf design have been divided with parallel and converging lines to make it suitable for this method

Italian quilting, also known as corded quilting, is characterized by the parallel lines of stitching, usually backstitched in a sewing cotton similar in colour to the top fabric. Quilting wool or thick, soft knitting wool is threaded in between the lines of stitching from the reverse side to raise the lines into relief. Like trapunto quilting, with which it can be effectively combined, this technique is only suitable for projects where the backing fabric is concealed, such as cushion tops, or items which are lined. Choose a slightly pliable fabric which will accommodate the cording.

MATERIALS
Top fabric Plain lightweight cotton, lawn, fine calico; silk dupion, twill, and shantung; fine woollens and jerseys
Filling Quilting, thick tapestry or knitting wool
Backing Lightweight cotton, lawn or fine calico

THREADS
Quilting thread, sewing cotton

NEEDLES
Betweens or an embroidery needle, large-eyed knitting wool needle

1 Mark the design on the top fabric using stencils, templates, dressmaker's carbon paper, or direct tracing.

2 Tack up the two layers in a grid pattern.

3 Frame up the work.

4 Stitch along the lines of the design with backstitch, or running stitch.

5 Slightly loosen the tension of the work in the frame, so that the surface is pliable. Thread the quilting wool on to a large-eyed needle and insert it from the back, sliding it between the stitched lines. Make sure that you do not pierce the top fabric. Bring the needle out again through the backing fabric and reinsert it through the same hole to continue.

6 Leave the quilting wool loosely tensioned to avoid puckering at sharp curves. Snip off both ends.

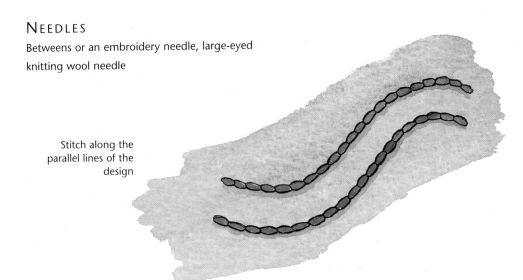

Stitch along the parallel lines of the design

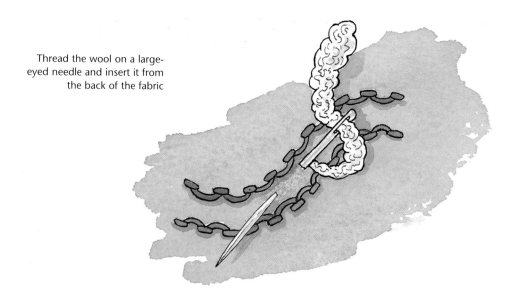

Thread the wool on a large-eyed needle and insert it from the back of the fabric

MACHINE METHOD

The raised channels of Italian quilting can be achieved by machine in several different ways.

The first method is simply to stitch two adjacent rows of machine stitching. The quilting wool is threaded in the same way as for the hand method.

A quicker and more accurate way is to use twin needles, spaced at either ⅛ or ³⁄₁₆in (3 or 4mm) apart. Thread up each needle as normal, keeping the threads untwisted and separated by the thread tension disc. Refer to your machine manual regarding stitching. Thread the quilting wool from the back by hand.

EQUIPMENT

Foot Embroidery foot
Needle Twin needle

DESIGNS

Italian quilting relies for its effect on a series of raised lines. Choose a design which includes curves or straight lines. Sharp corners are more difficult to carry out successfully. Suitable designs include interlaced Celtic patterns, the sinuous curves of the Art Nouveau period, and plant forms with curling or trailing stems. Wadded quilting designs can often be adapted by adding a second line parallel to the main line.

SHADOW QUILTING

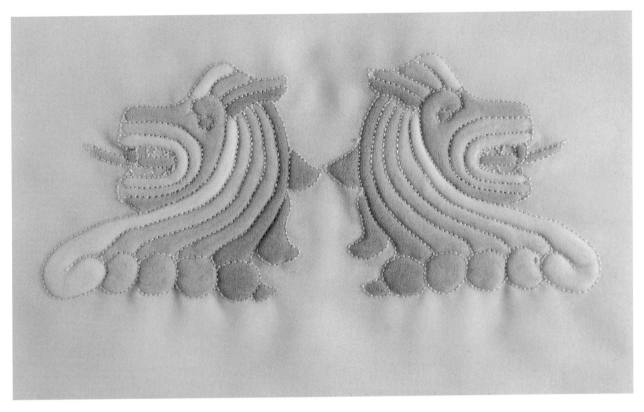

A mirror image design on chiffon, filled with hand-dyed quilting wool

Various methods of quilting can be modified using transparent fabric, giving a pretty delicate effect with soft tones. Both Italian quilting and trapunto quilting methods can be adapted for shadow quilting. Shadow quilting uses a visible filling. The top fabric can be white. A coloured one will not only mute the density of the filling and backing, but will also change its colour. Experiment with the colours of the top fabric, backing and filling to get the desired effect.

SHADOW ITALIAN QUILTING

Shadow Italian quilting is worked in a similar way to Italian quilting, but with strong coloured wools inserted in the channels, which show through the transparent fabric as delicate shadowy lines. The designs suitable for Italian quilting can also be used for shadow Italian quilting.

MATERIALS

Top fabric Light coloured transparent fabrics such as organza, organdie, net, chiffon and nylon

Filling Strongly coloured quilting wool, thick tapestry or knitting wool

Backing Lightweight cotton, lawn or fine calico.

THREADS

Quilting thread, sewing cotton

NEEDLES

Betweens or an embroidery needle, large-eyed knitting wool needle

1 Mark the design on the backing fabric using stencils, templates, dressmaker's carbon paper, or direct tracing.

2 Tack up the two layers in a grid pattern.

3 Frame up the work.

4 Stitch along the lines of the design with backstitch or running stitch.

5 Slightly loosen the tension of the work in the frame, so that the surface is pliable. Thread the quilting wool on to a large-eyed needle and insert it from the back, sliding it between the stitched lines. Make sure that you do not pierce the top fabric. Bring the needle out again through the backing fabric and reinsert it through the same hole to continue.

6 Leave the quilting wool loosely tensioned so as to avoid puckering at sharp curves. Snip off both ends.

MACHINE METHOD

The machine method for shadow Italian quilting is worked in a similar way to regular Italian quilting by machine (see page 48).

EQUIPMENT

Foot Embroidery foot

Needle Twin needle

SHADOW TRAPUNTO QUILTING

Conventional trapunto quilting can be adapted using a transparent top fabric combined with a filling of coloured wadding or wool. Designs suitable for trapunto quilting can be used for shadow trapunto.

1 Mark the design and prepare the layers as for shadow Italian quilting.

2 Stitch around the motif.

3 Insert coloured wadding or wool into the motif from the back of the work.

SHADOW QUILTING USING A VISIBLE FILLING

This third method of shadow quilting uses a visible filling, such as felt or heavy wool fabric shapes, which are placed between the backing fabric and the transparent top layer, giving a slightly raised effect. This technique is most suitable for panels, wallhangings or pictures as felt cannot be washed satisfactorily. However there is plenty of scope for adapting wadded quilting designs, or for using innovative ideas of your own.

MATERIALS

Top fabric Light coloured transparent fabrics such as organza, organdie, net, chiffon, and nylon

Filling Strongly coloured felt, wool or similar thick fabric

Backing Lightweight cotton, lawn or fine calico

THREADS

Quilting thread, sewing cotton

NEEDLES

Betweens or embroidery needle

The bold shapes of this organdie-covered shell design are simple to cut out in felt of different colours

1 Mark the design on the backing fabric using stencils, templates, dressmaker's carbon paper, or direct tracing.

2 Frame up the work.

3 Cut out the felt or wool motif and tack it in place on the backing, making sure that the knot is underneath and the marked lines are covered.

4 Pin and tack the transparent fabric on top, aligning the grain. Stitch around the felt motif with running, back or a decorative stitch. Remove the tacking stitches.

MACHINE METHOD

The machine method is worked in a similar way to the hand method.

EQUIPMENT

Foot Regular or embroidery foot
Needle Size 90–100

DESIGNS

Wadded quilting designs can be adapted for this method with bold shapes cut out in the visible filling fabric. More intricate ideas, such as landscapes, narrative pictures or still life designs also work well, with the felt shapes mounted on the backing like a jigsaw puzzle.

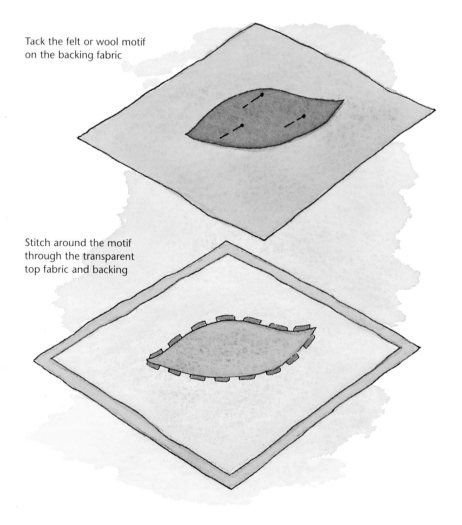

Tack the felt or wool motif on the backing fabric

Stitch around the motif through the transparent top fabric and backing

ENTRAPPING

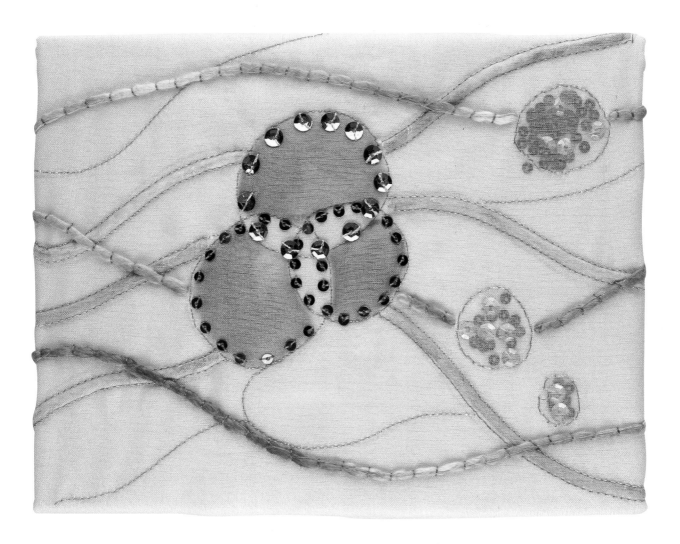

A development of shadow quilting involves entrapping small decorative items, such as beads, sequins, or snippets of fabric and felt in small pockets between layers of transparent fabric. This is a purely decorative technique, suitable for accessories, such as scarves, and small pieces of textile jewellery such as pendants or earrings. Framed panels with entrapped keepsakes can be stitched by hand or machine. The items for entrapping can be bonded or stuck to the background fabric or be left loose. Any kind of lightweight material can be entrapped.

This machine-quilted sample includes sequins entrapped in the circular shapes, shadow Italian and trapunto quilting with hand-dyed wools

MATERIALS

Top fabric Transparent fabrics such as organza, organdie, net, chiffon, and nylon

Filling Sequin shapes, such as hearts, stars, flowers; snippets of ribbon, felt, fabric, dried flowers, beads, tiny keepsakes

Backing As for top fabric

THREADS

Sewing cotton, embroidery threads

NEEDLES

Betweens or an embroidery needle

1 Mark the design on the transparent backing fabric by direct tracing.

2 Frame up the backing fabric.

3 Place or stick the sequins, beads and snippets of fabric in the areas where the pockets are to be created.

4 Pin and tack the transparent fabric on top, aligning the grain. Stitch along the marked lines to form the pockets with running, back or a decorative stitch, either by hand or machine.

MACHINE METHOD

The machine method is worked in a similar way to the hand method. The stitching can be straight, zigzag or automatic patterns.

EQUIPMENT

Foot Regular or embroidery foot
Needle Size 90–100

DESIGNS

Abstract or geometric patterns work best for this technique, including all-over repeat patterns such as those used for wadded quilting.

Right
Place or stick the sequins on the backing fabric

Far right
Stitch along the marked lines to form pockets

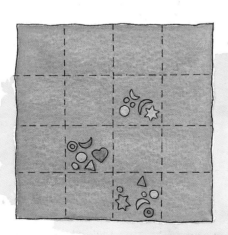

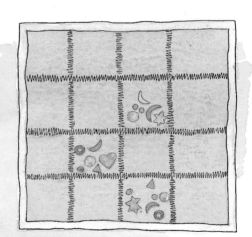

MACHINE QUILTING

Mushroom design cushion with vermicelli pattern machine quilting in silver metallic thread

Although hand stitching can be one of the joys of quilting, using a sewing machine will help to speed up the process. In fact, it is possible to work most hand-quilting techniques and designs by machine, provided a few adjustments are made. Modern sewing machines come with different attachments (see page 5), so you should refer to your handbook for any special instructions.

As with hand quilting, care should be taken with the preparation and tacking up to ensure that the work retains its shape and does not distort despite not being mounted in a frame. For all-over designs always stitch in the same direction, from

Layers of fabric applied, cut away and quilted with metallic threads in a narrow zigzag stitch (designed by Elspeth Kemp)

Hand-made felt with automatic stitches flat quilting along the lines of the surface texture

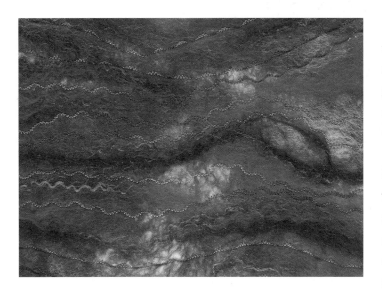

Although it is usual to machine quilt using a long stitch similar to backstitch, zigzag and satin stitch can also be used to great effect when more defined lines are required. Automatic stitches can also be effective, particularly on plain fabrics.

COUCH QUILTING

This method requires the couching thread to be threaded through the hole in an embroidery or braiding foot, so that it is automatically fed through and held by the machine stitching.

EQUIPMENT
Foot Embroidery or braiding foot
Needle Size 90–100

top to bottom, starting at the centre top and working towards the sides. For informal designs start in the centre and work outwards.

6 THINKING ABOUT DESIGN

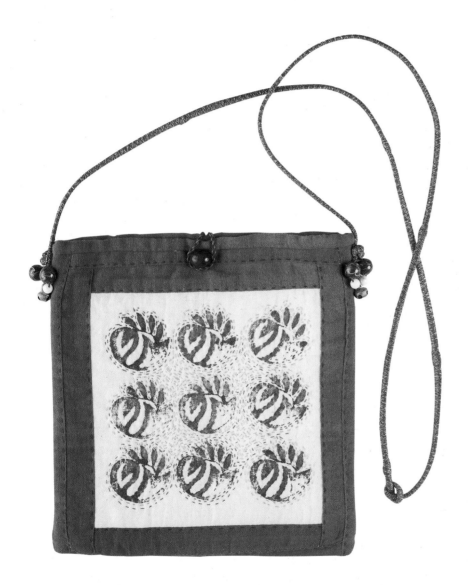

Bag, by Shirley Isaacs
Repeat motif wood-
block print, quilted
with running stitches
and seeding and
finished with log cabin
border, bead tassels
and machine-made
cord

Designing your own quilting can add great enjoyment to your needlework. Ideas can be taken from traditional sources by reproducing the patterns of the past, or you can develop your own ideas from drawings or photographs. You will need to adapt the original motifs so that they are suitable for your chosen quilting technique, for example making parallel lines for Italian quilting or simplifying complex patterns for wadded quilting. Try experimenting on small samples.

BACKGROUNDS

All-over background patterns are the most popular way of holding the fabric and wadding layers together. They can be used alone or more effectively surround motifs or focal points in the design. Simple stripes, checks or diamonds can be drawn using a marker and ruler, either directly on to the fabric, or on to squared paper.

Patchwork templates are useful aids for constructing simple patterns of hexagons, scallops, circles or rectangles.

TRADITIONAL MOTIFS AND BORDERS

Specialist quilting shops sell a wide range of quilting stencils and templates which can be used individually, repeated or combined with backgrounds or other motifs.

A border can be an important feature in a project, particularly a large item such as a quilt. It can be made with simple lines or individual motifs repeated, mirrored or reversed. Traditional continuous borders include cables, twists and feathers.

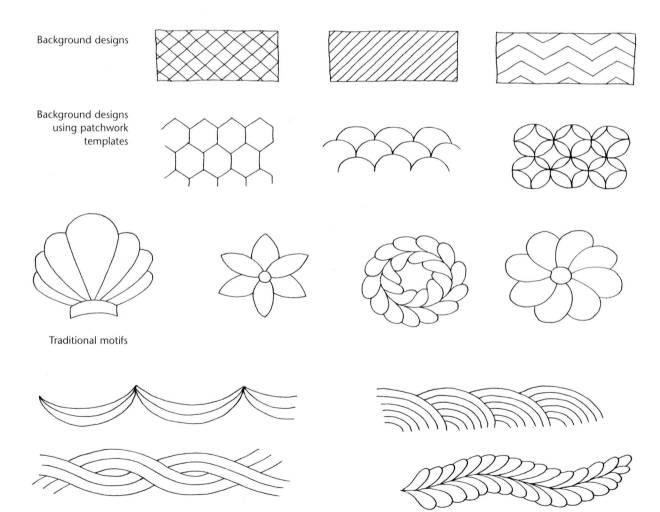

Background designs

Background designs using patchwork templates

Traditional motifs

Traditional borders

PRINCIPLES OF PATTERN

Arranging and repeating single motifs or units to form a pattern is an essential ingredient of quilting design. Repeat motifs can be used for backgrounds, borders or as the focal point in a design.

You can arrange a single unit in a variety of ways – straight, half drop, brick or random. It can be mirrored, overlapped, reversed or grouped in a circle, square or abstract shape.

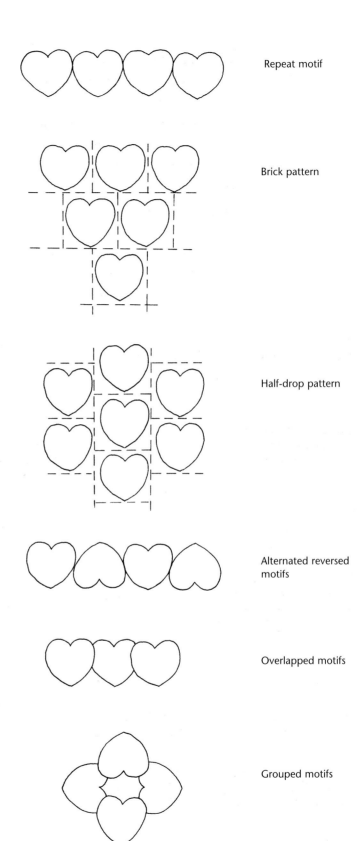

Repeat motif

Brick pattern

Half-drop pattern

Alternated reversed motifs

Overlapped motifs

Grouped motifs

7 HOME FURNISHING PROJECTS

Decorating your home with beautiful soft furnishings is one of the joys of being creative. Quilting is a technique which lends itself to large-scale projects, such as quilts or wall hangings, suitable for the experienced stitcher. If you are a beginner, you can give full rein to your imagination when making small accessories, such as cushions, table mats and kitchen equipment covers, which can be quilted using a variety of different methods.

QUILT-AS-YOU-GO BOLSTER CUSHION

A selection of strips of furnishing or dress fabrics can be turned into an attractive bolster cushion to grace your sofa, chaise longue or bed. The measurements given are for an 18in (45cm) long bolster and the number and length of strips given is only a guide, they can be cut to whatever width you wish. Choose a fabric with a large motif for the end circles and work trapunto quilting to give texture to this area.

MATERIALS AND EQUIPMENT

Cotton backing fabric, 19 x 25in (48 x 64cm)

4oz wadding, 19 x 25in (48 x 64cm)

Strips of furnishing or dress fabric in a variety of widths from 3–4in (8–10cm);
 and the following lengths 1 x 34in (86cm), 2 x 31in (79cm), 2 x 26in (66cm),
 2 x 23in (59cm), 2 x 18in (45cm), 2 x 13in (33cm), 2 x 9in (23cm)

8in (20cm) diameter circle of printed fabric with large central motif

8in (20cm) diameter circle of cotton backing fabric

Scraps of wadding for stuffing

2 bias strips in toning fabrics, 25 x 1½in (64 x 4cm)

Piping cord, 2 lengths each 25in (64cm) long

10in (25cm) zip (if desired)

18in (45cm) long bolster cushion

Sewing machine and piping foot

Basic sewing equipment

PREPARATION

1   Tack the wadding to the backing in a grid pattern (see page 21).

QUILT-AS-YOU-GO

2   Pin and stitch the first strip, right side up, diagonally across the centre of the wadding and backing, from corner to corner.

3   Put the second strip right side down onto the first. Pin, tack the strip into place and sew through both strips, wadding and backing. Turn the second strip right side up and press the seam flat. Carry on attaching strips until you reach the corner of the backing fabric, then work out from the centre again, covering the other half.

4   Stitch along the edge of the quilted piece to secure the ends of the strips.

TRAPUNTO QUILTING THE END PIECES

5   Tack the printed fabric circles to their backing fabrics.

6   Machine stitch or backstitch around the motif to enclose the areas to be stuffed.

7   Slit the backing fabric and stuff it with wadding, making sure that the wadding is pushed firmly into all the points of the motif. Sew up the slits in the backing fabric.

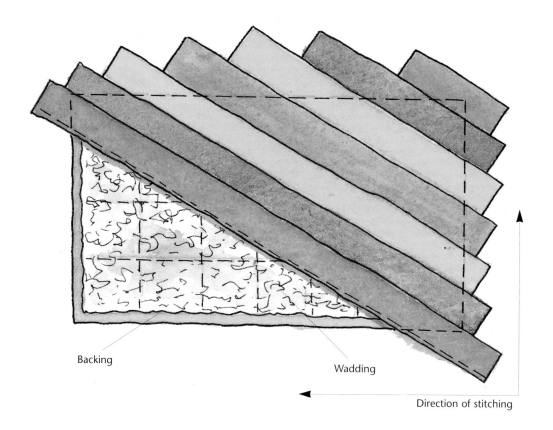

Backing

Wadding

Direction of stitching

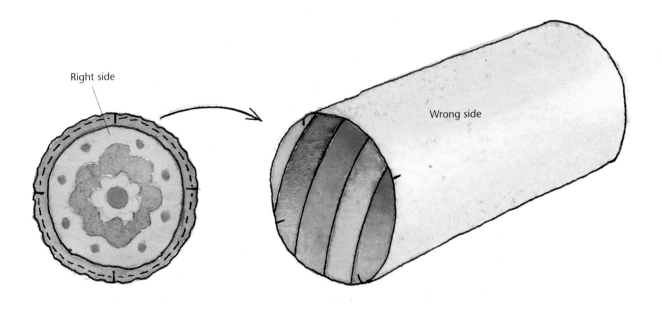

Right side

Wrong side

MAKING UP

8 Pin the shorter edges of the rectangle right side together, tack and sew the seam leaving a 10in (25cm) gap to insert the cushion pad through. If you are using a zip, insert it at this point. Press the seam flat and finish with zigzag stitch along the seam edges to stop them fraying.

9 Mark the edges of the circle pieces and the main body of the cushion at four equidistant points, dividing the circle into equal quarters.

10 Prepare the piping (see page 30) and stitch it around edge of the circles with the raw edges aligned.

11 With the right sides together, pin the circles into the ends of the cushion,

matching up the four marked points. Tack and stitch the pieces in place, making sure that the piping is held tightly into the seam. Stitch with a piping foot attached to the machine.

12 Turn the cushion cover through to the right side, and insert the cushion pad. Close the zip or stitch up the gap by hand.

VARIATIONS

To adjust to a different sized cushion, measure the length, adding 1in (2.5cm) for seam allowances, and then measure the circumference, adding seam allowances as before. Cut the backing and wadding to these measurements.

Instead of working trapunto quilting at either end, stitch large tassels for an attractive finishing touch.

CAFETIERE COSY AND MATCHING NAPKINS

Impress your dinner guests or casual visitors with this machine quilted cafetiere cosy and matching napkins. Choose washable fabrics with a bold design which can be simply accented with machine couching in toning thread. The cosy is reversible, so you can coordinate the colours to match both your best dinner service and everyday coffee mugs.

CAFETIERE COSY
MATERIALS AND EQUIPMENT

Patterned fabric, 14½ x 7in (37 x 18cm)

Plain fabric, 14½ x 7in (37 x 18cm)

2oz wadding, 14½ x 7in (37 x 18cm)

Contrasting bias binding or fabric trim, 2 x 46in (5 x 118cm)

Fabric marker

Ruler

Soft embroidery thread in two colours

Matching sewing cotton

Contrast sewing cotton

Clear invisible thread

2 Velcro spots

Large-eyed needle

Basic sewing equipment

Sewing machine with braiding foot

Preparing the fabric

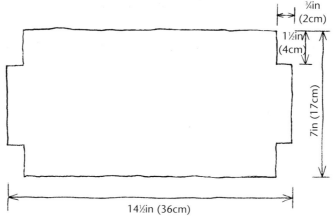

¾in
(2cm)

1½in
(4cm)

7in (17cm)

14½in (36cm)

PREPARATION

1   Cut a rectangle off the corners of the top fabric, backing and wadding, 1½in (4cm) in height and ¾in (2cm) in width.

2   Mark the lines of the design on the patterned fabric you wish to emphasize with couching.

3   Pin and tack the three layers together with the right sides of the fabric outermost and the wadding sandwiched between, as for wadded quilting (see page 31).

MACHINE QUILTING

4   Thread up the bobbin of the machine with thread which contrasts with the backing fabric (tan in this case). Machine couch quilt with soft embroidery thread and matching colour top thread (see page 58 for more details) along the lines of the printed design, starting at the centre top. Stitch each line in the same direction.

5   Turn the work to the wrong side. Thread a contrasting soft embroidery cotton onto a large-eyed needle and thread it under the zigzag machine stitching so it is visible.

BINDING AND FASTENING

6   Prepare the binding and stitch it around the edge of the cosy (see page 29). Snip the seam allowance into the stitching lines at the corners and join the two ends on the diagonal (see page 29).

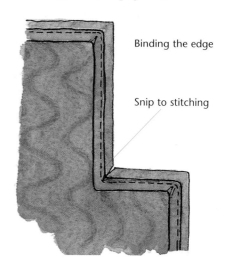

Binding the edge

Snip to stitching

7 Fold the binding to the back. Turn under, press the raw edge of the binding and slip stitch in place.

8 Using invisible thread, machine zigzag two Velcro spots on the right side of the lap-over flap and the other halves on the reverse at the other end of the cover.

NAPKINS
MATERIALS AND
EQUIPMENT

Plain fabric, 12 x 12in (30 x 30cm) for each napkin

Patterned fabric, 5in (13cm) sided right-angled triangle for corner trim

2oz wadding, 5in (13cm) sided right-angled triangle

Fabric marker

Basic sewing kit

Sewing machine and braiding foot

MAKING UP

1 Pin and tack the triangle of wadding to the back of the triangle of printed fabric. Mark a ½in (1cm) seam allowance on the diagonal side.

2 Mark a point 4½in (11.5cm) from one corner of the napkin on two adjacent sides. With right sides together, place the triangle on the napkin with marks aligned and with the point facing towards the centre. Machine stitch the triangle to the napkin along the diagonal edge (see above).

3 Trim the wadding to the seam and fold back the triangle to meet the corner. Press and tack in place.

4 Couch quilt along the printed design as for the cafetiere cover.

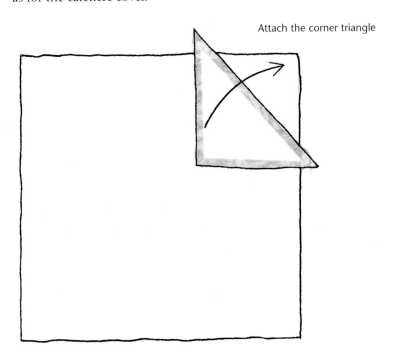

Attach the corner triangle

5 Neaten the edge by machine stitching with a medium-width zigzag around the perimeter of the napkin and the triangle trim. Fold over the hem and stitch with a row of straight stitches.

VARIATIONS

Couch quilt narrow ribbon in straight lines on plain or striped fabric. Add piping (see page 30) or a frill for a different finishing touch.

Make decorative fastenings such as buttons or bows for added interest.

CONTEMPORARY CALICO CUSHION

Tied quilting is often used as a simple and invisible method for holding layers of fabric and wadding together. This calico cushion is given a modern approach by making a feature of the pearl cotton ties. The button fastening completes the effect.

MATERIALS AND EQUIPMENT

Calico or natural linen, 2 pieces 19 x 13in (48 x 33cm)

Calico or natural linen, 1 piece 13 x 6½in (33 x 16cm)

4oz wadding, 19 x 13in (48 x 33cm)

Cotton backing fabric, 1 piece 19 x 13in (48 x 33cm)

Pearl cotton no.3 in blue, beige and brown

Sewing cotton in blue and cream

Pair of pliers

Large-eyed wool needle

Fabric marker

Three 1⅛in (2.9cm) buttons or button moulds for covering

Sewing machine

Basic sewing equipment

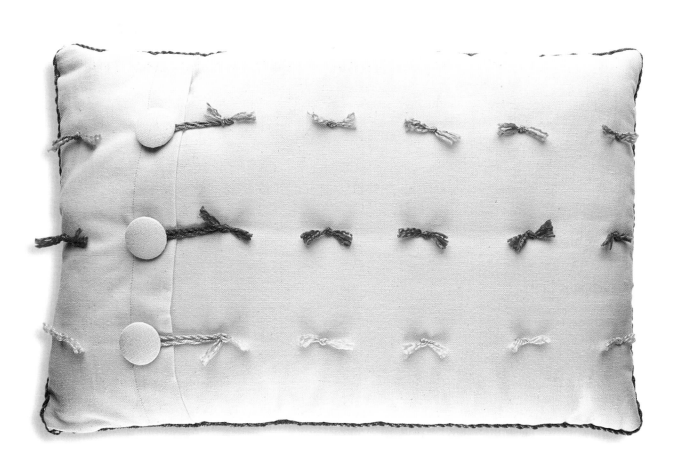

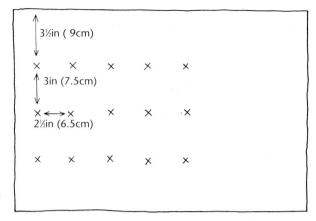

3½in (9cm)

× × × × ×

3in (7.5cm)

× ←→× × × · ×
2½in (6.5cm)

× × × × ×

Position of ties

×

×

×

Flap

PREPARATION

1   Following the diagram, mark the grid of 15 dots, in three rows of five, for the ties on one piece of calico. Mark three dots for the ties on the flap (see above).

QUILTING

2   Assemble the three layers of calico, wadding and backing, pin and tack as for tied quilting (see page 42).

3   For each tie, cut three 5in (13cm) lengths of pearl cotton. Thread the three lengths together on the large-eyed needle and tie at the marked spot. Use the pliers to help pull the thread through the layers of wadding and fabric. Fray out the ends to form a fluffy tassel and trim to ½in (1cm).

MAKING THE FLAP

4   Stitch a 1in (2.5cm) hem along one long edge and work three ties on marked dots. With the right sides together stitch the flap to the cushion back, matching up the raw edges (see below).

MAKING UP

5   Neaten the opening side of cushion front with a zigzag stitch.

6   With right sides together, stitch the front to the back of the cushion along three sides, leaving the flap end open to turn the work through (see opposite).

7   Trim the wadding to the seam and the excess fabric from the corners. Turn

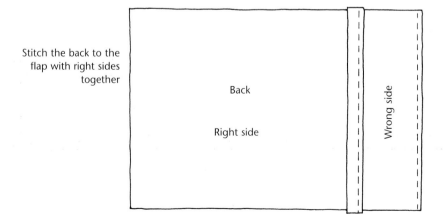

Stitch the back to the flap with right sides together

Back

Right side

Wrong side

through to the right side, folding the flap to the front.

CORDS AND FINISHING

8   Cover the button moulds with calico or use purchased buttons, and stitch them in place on the flap.

9   Make three cords (see page 30) for button loops, using two strands of pearl cotton each 15in (38cm) in blue, beige and brown and one cord for the outer edge using two strands of blue pearl cotton each 140in (360cm) long.

10   Stitch the long cord to the seam between the front and back of the cushion, pushing the ends through to the back at one corner and knotting to secure.

11   For the button loops, thread the cord on the large-eyed needle and bring it through to the front of the work, adjacent to the tie, nearest to the flap. Insert the needle close by and tie to secure at the back of the work, forming a loop which fits the button fastening.

VARIATIONS

Instead of tie quilting with thread, stitch the layers together using large wooden, china or glass beads.

For a more luxurious effect, choose velvet, brocade or satin, adding a frill to the flap and tying with metallic threads.

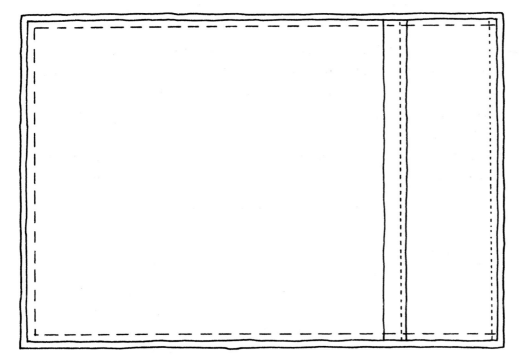

Stitch the front to the back, leaving the end open

PLACE MATS WITH FEATHER DESIGN

Feather designs appear in many traditional quilts, both American and British, and are mainly stitched by hand. For a coordinated effect choose washable fabrics which will harmonize with your plates. Remember that most wadding is not heatproof, so the place mats should be used in conjunction with a heatproof mat underneath.

MATERIALS AND EQUIPMENT

Cotton fabric, 2 pieces 16 x 12in (40 x 30cm) for each place mat

2oz wadding, 16 x 12in (40 x 30cm) for each place mat

Printed cotton fabric bias strip for binding each mat, 42 x 1½in (107 x 4cm)

Matching sewing cotton

Quilting thread in toning colour

Tracing paper and pencil

Dressmaker's carbon and spent ballpoint pen

Basic sewing equipment

PREPARATION

1 Fold a sheet of tracing paper in four. Enlarge the template by 154% using a photocopier. Trace the enlarged template on one quarter and retrace the other three quarters to make up the oval shape.

2 Cut two ovals of fabric and one piece of wadding for each place mat.

3 Enlarge the feather design by 154% on a photocopier and transfer it to the top fabric, using dressmaker's carbon paper (see page 14). Mark a line 2in (5cm) in from the edge all the way around the oval.

QUILTING

4 Assemble the three layers of top fabric, backing and wadding, pin and tack for wadded quilting (see page 21).

5 If you wish you can mount the work in a frame, but the small scale of this project means that it can be satisfactorily stitched in the hand. Work running stitch along the feather design and border which you have marked.

BINDING

6 Bind around the edge of the oval with a contrasting binding (see page 29). Be careful to ease the binding around curves, otherwise the binding will pucker when pressed after stitching.

VARIATIONS

These place mats can be made reversible, if you use different fabrics for front and back. For a densely quilted design, quilt the entire background with an all-over pattern, such as diamonds, chevrons, scallops or squares.

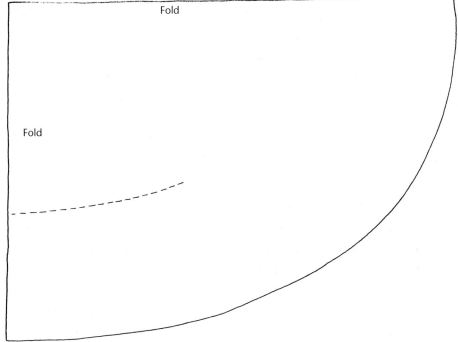
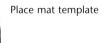

Fold

Fold

Place mat template

Enlarge by 154%

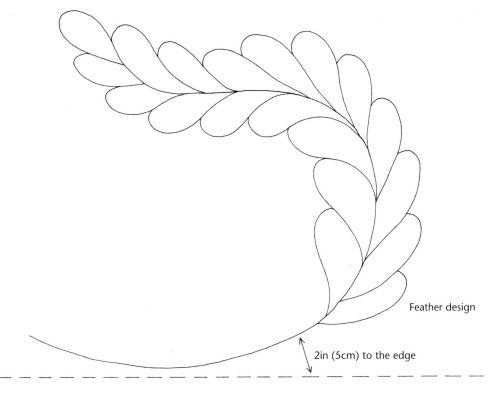

Feather design

2in (5cm) to the edge

Enlarge by 154%

8 GIFTS

Making a present for a special occasion or for a good friend will undoubtedly give both you and the recipient great pleasure. Gifts can be small personalized items or, on a larger scale, can include cushions or even quilts. A tiny padded pin cushion would be treasured by a keen needlewoman, a shadow quilted landscape can remind your family of a happy holiday.

PILLOW QUILTING WALLHANGING

Wallhangings can be any size and this small example will

fit in most rooms. Made from scraps of silk, it has a

sophisticated effect which can harmonize with the colour scheme

of your living room or that of a lucky friend. It consists of 13

individually padded sections, which are stitched together, quilted

and finished with a top band and decorative tassels.

MATERIALS AND EQUIPMENT

13 rectangles of 3in (8cm) wide different coloured silk, the largest being 10½in (26.5cm) long
Rectangle of silk, 14½ x 2½in (37 x 6.5cm) for top band
Silk backing fabric, 24 x 20in (61 x 51cm)
Fusible fleece, 24 x 20in (61 x 51cm)
Pearl cotton no.8 for quilting
Pearl cotton no.5 in four colours for tassels
Piece of card, 3½ x 4in (9 x 10cm)
Sewing cotton
Squared drafting paper and pencil
Sewing machine
Flat aluminium strip or wooden lath 13in x ½in (33 x 1cm)
Two curtain rings
Basic sewing equipment

PREPARATION

1   Make a paper pattern for the 13 pieces using the measurements given on the template. Add turnings to all the edges.

2   Using the paper patterns cut out the following pieces from different coloured silks: 2 x A, 2 x B, 2 x C, 1 x D, 1 x E, 2 x F, 2 x G and 1 x H.

3   Cut out backing and fusible fleece for each piece. Cut out a fusible fleece piece for the top band.

PILLOW QUILTING

4   Make all thirteen pillows in a similar way. Using a damp cloth, press the fusible fleece to the wrong side of the top fabric. Place the right sides together on the backing fabric and stitch round three sides, leaving the top side open, through which you can turn the work (see below).

5   Peel the fleece away from the edge of the fabric and trim it to the seam. Trim the corners and points to remove bulk.

6   Turn through to the right side and press lightly. Press the opening to the inside and oversew to close the gap.

FINISHING

7   Oversew the sections with their right sides together.

8   Back the top band of fabric with fusible fleece. With right sides together, stitch the band across the top of the hanging (see below). Fold in the ends, fold the band to the back and stitch it to the back of the work to form a channel, through which to thread the aluminium strip or lath, when ready for hanging.

Make the pillows   Leave the end open

Stitch the band to the top of the wallhanging

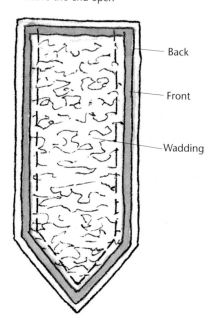

Back

Front

Wadding

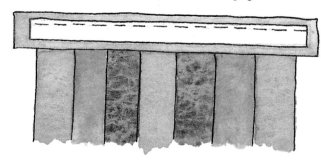

Make seven tassels

Wind the cotton around the card 20 times

Stitch the tassel to the point of the wallhanging

Pillow quilting wallhanging template

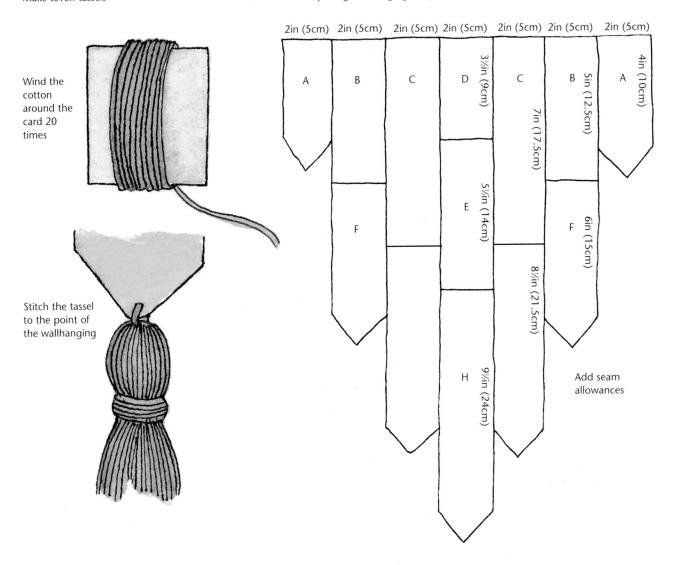

2in (5cm) 2in (5cm) 2in (5cm) 2in (5cm) 2in (5cm) 2in (5cm) 2in (5cm)

A   B   C   D   C   B   A

3½in (9cm)

7in (17.5cm)

5in (12.5cm)

4in (10cm)

F

E

F

6in (15cm)

5½in (14cm)

8½in (21.5cm)

H

9½in (24cm)

Add seam allowances

9 With pearl cotton, work contour quilting (see page 34) in running stitch around each section.

10 Make seven tassels by winding pearl cotton 20 times round a piece of card. Cut through the loop at the bottom. Thread up a second piece of pearl cotton and wind it around the loop ½in (1cm) from the top to form the head. Using the same thread, stitch the tassel to the points of the wallhanging.

11 Insert the aluminium strip or lath, stitch up the ends and sew on the curtain rings at the back at either end.

VARIATIONS

For a larger-scale hanging, simply double or treble the size of the sections. For a children's room, choose brightly coloured or patterned fabrics.

ART NOUVEAU
PHOTO FRAME

Photo frames or mirrors are always acceptable gifts and this
Italian quilted version with its sinuous Art Nouveau design is
no exception. The stitching in pearl cotton gives the effect of
tiny beads outlining the design and the larger areas are
trapunto quilted. Small details are worked in quilting thread
and the handmade cord gives a professional finishing touch.

MATERIALS AND EQUIPMENT

Green furnishing fabric, 2 pieces 14 x 14in (35 x 35cm)
Backing cotton, 14 x 14in (35 x 35cm)
Green pearl cotton no.5
Green quilting thread
Quilting wool and large-eyed needle
12in (30cm) quilting or embroidery hoop
Tracing paper
White dressmaker's carbon paper and spent ballpoint pen
Mounting board, 2 pieces 7½ x 9¼in (19 x 23.5cm)
Craft knife, rule and cutting board
Fabric glue
Pair of pliers
Circular needle
Basic sewing equipment

PREPARATION

1   Enlarge the design template by 125% on a photocopier and transfer it to one piece of green fabric using dressmaker's carbon paper (see page 4).

2   Tack the fabric to the backing fabric and mount it in a frame.

QUILTING

3   Using pearl cotton, backstitch (see page 25) along the main lines of the design and complete the dotted lines with quilting thread.

4   Insert the quilting wool between the parallel lines as for Italian quilting (see page 50) and fill in the larger areas with trapunto quilting (see page 47).

FINISHING

5   Cut a curved top edge on both pieces of card following the pattern and an aperture in one piece of card, leaving a 1¾in (4.5cm) wide border all round.

6   To prepare the quilted photo frame, trim the fabric to the size of the card with the aperture, leaving ¾in (2cm) extra all around. (Do not cut out the centre at this point.)

7   Position the card centrally on the wrong side of the fabric and trim the corners diagonally to reduce bulk. Snip the curves at the top edge. Spread a small amount of fabric glue along the side edges of the card and fold over the fabric so that it is stretched taut and held firmly in

place. Repeat the process, gluing the top and bottom edges in place (see below left).

8   Cut out the central window from the fabric, cutting ¾in (2cm) in from the edge of the card. Carefully make diagonal cuts at the corners. Apply the fabric glue to the back of the card as before and fold over the fabric to the back as before. Cover the frame back with fabric in a similar way (see below right).

9   Using a circular needle and quilting thread, oversew the two pieces of fabric-covered card together, around three sides, leaving a space on one side through which to insert the photograph.

Below left
Position the card on the wrong side of the fabric and trim the corners to reduce the bulk

Below right
Cut out the central window and fold the fabric back onto the card

10   Make a twisted cord (see page 30) using three strands of pearl cotton each 100in (250cm) and oversew it around the edge, inserting the ends between the two pieces of card. Make a shorter length of cord in a similar way and stitch it to the back of the frame for hanging.

Design template
Enlarge by 125%

VARIATIONS

If you prefer to use this design for a mirror, use adhesive mirror mounts to secure it to the frame back.

This design would also be suitable for shadow Italian quilting, if you used a transparent fabric and coloured wools for the insertions.

CLEMATIS TRELLIS SILK CUSHION

Make this silk cushion, with its clematis flowers winding through the trellis background, to complement a pretty bedroom scheme or as a present for a special friend or relation. The dainty effect of the vermicelli pattern machine stitching is achieved with variegated threads set against lustrous pure silk dupion.

MATERIALS AND EQUIPMENT

White silk dupion, 2 pieces 16 x 16in (40 x 40cm)

White backing fabric, 16 x 16in (40 x 40cm)

2oz wadding, 16 x 16in (40 x 40cm)

Silk dupion bias strip, 1½ x 60in (4 x 153cm)

Piping cord, 60in (153cm)

Variegated machine embroidery thread in pink and green

White sewing cotton

Pink stranded embroidery cotton

Greaseproof paper and pencil

Sewing machine with appliqué foot, darning foot and piping foot

Large-eyed needle

14in (35cm) cushion pad

Basic sewing equipment

Design template
Enlarge by 350%

PREPARATION

1   Enlarge the design 350% on a photocopier and trace it onto grease-proof paper.

QUILTING

2   Assemble the three layers of silk, wadding and backing fabric. Pin and tack as for wadded quilting (see page 21). Position the design on top and tack in place (see page 33).

3   With the appliqué foot attached to the machine, stitch through all the layers along the marked outlines of the design using pink variegated thread for the flowers and green for the remainder. Omit the centres of the flowers.

4   Tear away the greaseproof paper and take the ends of thread through to the back of the work using a large-eyed needle. Fasten off the ends.

MACHINE EMBROIDERY

5   For the flower centres in pink and vermicelli shading in green, disengage the feed dogs and set the stitch width and length to 0. Remove the normal presser foot and substitute a darning foot.

6   Lower the presser bar and bring both threads to the surface of the fabric. Stitch in a circular movement to make the centre of the flowers, and then stitch small lines radiating outwards for the petals (see opposite).

Centre of the flowers

Vermicelli stitch

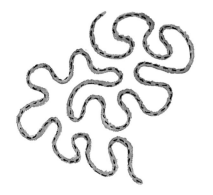

10 Turn through to the right side, insert the cushion pad and stitch up the gap.

11 Using two strands of pink embroidery cotton, oversew the piping with stitches spaced ½in (1cm) apart (see below).

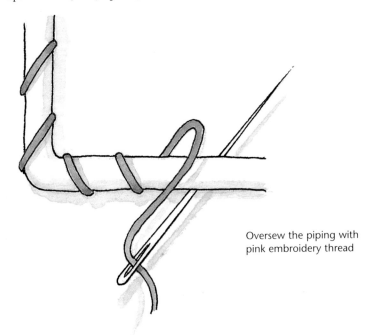

Oversew the piping with pink embroidery thread

7 For the vermicelli shading, stitch in a series of tiny loops and curves.

FINISHING

8 Machine stitch around the edge and cut away the excess wadding. Make piping and attach around the perimeter (see page 30).

9 With right sides together, stitch the cushion back to the quilted front, leaving a gap through which to turn the work.

VARIATIONS

This design can be adapted by substituting Italian quilting for the trellis and trapunto quilting for the flowers.

It can also be used for a shadow quilted project, by using transparent fabric with a coloured infill.

This technique can be used for a more contemporary designs by choosing different fabrics such as linen or cotton, combined with bolder coloured threads.

SHADOW QUILTED MOUNTAIN SCENE

Shadow quilting with felt lends itself to a variety of projects, especially framed pictures and panels which will not need to be laundered. Landscapes provide a simple subject with clearly defined areas. Choose strongly coloured felts and a transparent top fabric for the best effect.

MATERIALS AND EQUIPMENT

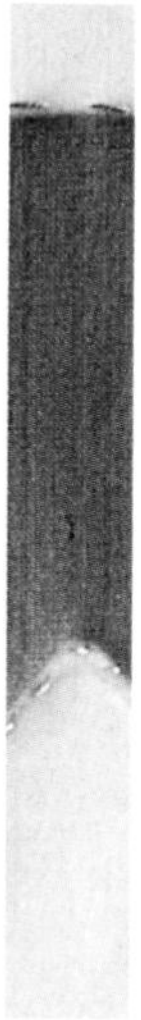

White cotton backing fabric, 16 x 14in (40 x 35cm)

White organdie or organza, 16 x 14in (40 x 35cm)

Stretcher frame, 15 x 13in (38 x 33cm) and drawing pins

Scraps of felt in royal blue, white, beige, emerald green, dark green, lime green, grey and tan

Tacking cotton

Matching embroidery threads as for felt

Stranded embroidery cotton in dark blue, mid blue, pale blue, dark green, emerald green and lime green

Tracing paper and pencil

Dressmaker's carbon paper and a spent ballpoint pen

Picture or photo frame with 10 x 8in (25 x 20cm) aperture

Mounting board, 10 x 8in (25 x 20cm)

Basic sewing equipment

Design template
Enlarge by 125%

Flower motif

PREPARATION

1   Enlarge the design by 125% on a photocopier and number each piece. Trace, and cut out the tracing to use as templates when cutting out the felt in the appropriate colours.

2   Mark the perimeter of the design in the middle of the backing fabric and mount it on a stretcher frame (see page 19).

SHADOW QUILTING

3   Assemble the felt pieces within the marked lines, like a jigsaw puzzle, and tack them in place to form the design.

4   Tack the transparent fabric over the felt and stitch around and between the felt shapes, using running stitch in the appropriate coloured thread. Remove the tacking stitches from the fabric.

EMBROIDERY

5   Copy the flower motif on to plain paper. Using dressmaker's carbon paper (see page 14), transfer the design to the top fabric.

6   The embroidery is worked throughout in two strands of stranded cotton. Work the gentian leaves in satin stitch (see below) in shades of green and the stalks in stem stitch (see over).

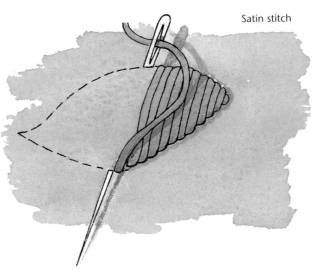

Satin stitch

Stem stitch

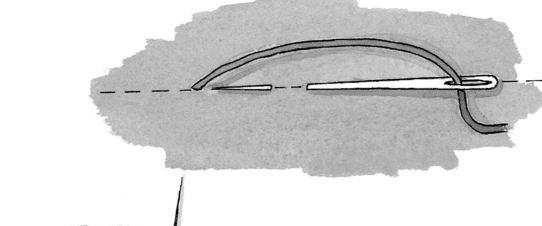

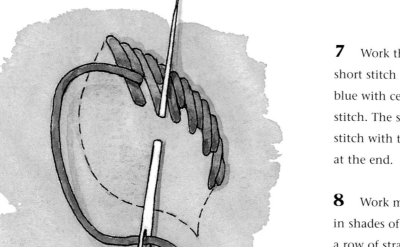

Long and short stitch

French knots

7 Work the gentian flowers in long and short stitch (see left) in dark blue and mid blue with central veins in green stem stitch. The stamens are in pale blue stem stitch with three French knots (see below) at the end.

8 Work more French knots (see below) in shades of green between the stones and a row of straight stitches along the line of the hillside.

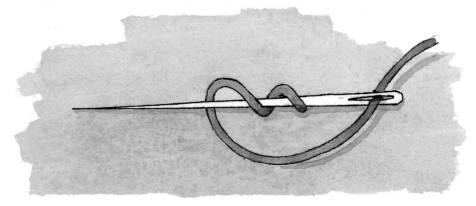

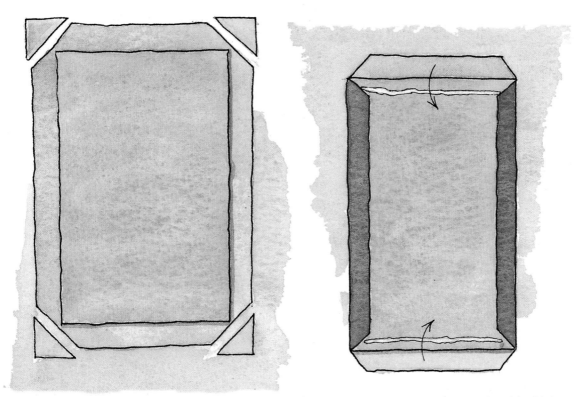

Trim the corners to reduce bulk

Fold over the edge of the fabric so that
it is held firmly in place

FINISHING

9 Trim the fabric to the size of the
mounting board leaving ⅜in (2cm) extra
all around. Position the card in the middle
of the wrong side of the fabric and trim
the corners diagonally to reduce bulk (see
above left). Spread a small amount of
fabric glue along the side edges of the card
and fold over the fabric so that it is
stretched taut and held firmly in place (see
above right). Repeat the process, gluing
the top and bottom edges in place.

10 Place the finished piece in the frame
and secure the back.

VARIATIONS

This design could be adapted for
machine quilting and combined
combined with a fabric-painted
background. Make your own design by
tracing and enlarging a photograph of a
favourite holiday haunt, view or even a
picture of your home. You could also use
your favourite flower as a motif.

9 ACCESSORIES

Accessories are ideal articles to make
for yourself, or to give as presents as
they are usually quick to make and
decorative to wear. Various methods of
quilting can be used for all types of
bags, from everyday handbags to
exotically embellished evening bags.
Wadded quilting makes an ideal trim
for collars, cuffs or lapels on garments,
and shadow quilting lends itself to
being used for delicate evening wear in
transparent fabrics.

SASHIKO TOTE BAG

Use this bag as a roomy handbag, shoulder bag or small carrier. The design combines a traditional Japanese pattern of scallops and basket weave in running stitch with butterflies outlined in backstitch.

MATERIALS AND EQUIPMENT

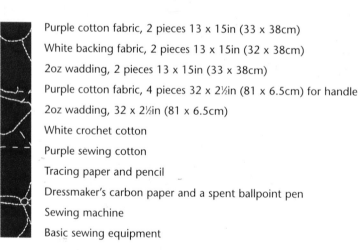

Purple cotton fabric, 2 pieces 13 x 15in (33 x 38cm)

White backing fabric, 2 pieces 13 x 15in (32 x 38cm)

2oz wadding, 2 pieces 13 x 15in (33 x 38cm)

Purple cotton fabric, 4 pieces 32 x 2½in (81 x 6.5cm) for handle

2oz wadding, 32 x 2½in (81 x 6.5cm)

White crochet cotton

Purple sewing cotton

Tracing paper and pencil

Dressmaker's carbon paper and a spent ballpoint pen

Sewing machine

Basic sewing equipment

PREPARATION

1 Enlarge the design by 200% (see opposite) and transfer it to one piece of purple fabric using dressmaker's carbon paper (see page 14).

2 Tack the top fabric, wadding and backing fabric so that it is ready for quilting (see page 21).

3 For the back, mark a vertical line in the centre and two sets of double vertical lines ½in (1cm) apart, 3in (8cm) from the centre. Tack the fabric to the wadding and backing as for the front.

SASHIKO QUILTING

4 Work the butterflies in backstitch (see pages 24–25) and the rest of the design in running stitch (see page 24) using crochet cotton. Work the lines on the back in running stitch.

HANDLES

5 With the right sides together, tack the fabric strip to the backing fabric with the wadding beneath. Machine stitch both long edges and turn through to the right side.

6 Work two rows of running stitch along the length of each handle.

MAKING UP

7 With right sides together, stitch up the side and bottom seams. Neaten the seams and top edge by overcasting by hand or machine.

8 To shape the base, keep the bag inside out and stitch across the corners at right angles to the side seams 2in (5cm) from the bottom (see page 108).

9 Stitch the resultant triangular shapes to the bottom seam.

Stitch the handles to the hem

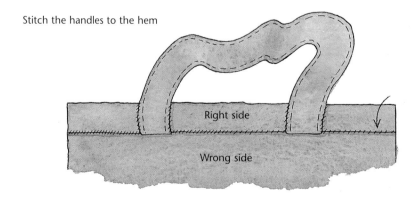

Right side

Wrong side

Design template
Enlarge by 200%

10 With raw edges together, pin the handles in place, matching the lines on the handles with the vertical lines on the bag.

11 Fold the top edge over to the inside with a 2in (5cm) hem and stitch in place. Stitch the handles to the hem (see below).

VARIATIONS

Adapt this design for a set of decorative place mats or a cushion.

To make the bag more secure, insert a zip in the opening.

COSMETICS BAG

Bags to hold toiletries and make-up are useful accessories for the bedroom, bathroom or handbag. Although not a usual method of quilting, machine stitching ribbon to wadded fabric gives a luxurious, yet quick to accomplish effect. You can line the bag with plastic-coated or washable fabric and choose materials to match your furnishings or clothes.

MATERIALS AND EQUIPMENT

Turquoise cotton fabric, 18 x 13in (45 x 33cm)

Turquoise cotton fabric, 2 bias strips 14 x 1¾in (35 x 4.5cm) for binding

2oz wadding, 18 x 13in (45 x 33cm)

Washable or plastic-coated lining, 18 x 13in (45 x 33cm)

Tartan ribbon, 5½ yards (5m) ½in (1cm) wide

Turquoise sewing thread

Red sewing thread

10in (25cm) zip

Sewing machine with appliqué foot

Tracing paper and pencil

Dressmaker's carbon paper and spent ballpoint pen

Basic sewing equipment

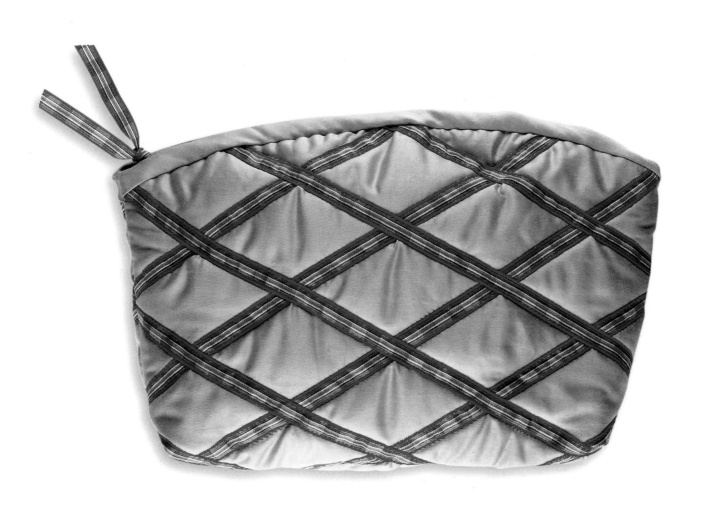

PREPARATION

1   Enlarge the template (see opposite) by 137% on a photocopier and add on seam allowances.

2   Cut out the fabric, wadding and backing.

3   Using dressmaker's carbon paper (see page 14), mark the lines for the ribbon appliqué on the top fabric.

4   Tack the three layers together for wadded quilting.

QUILTING

5   Cut the ribbon into lengths to fit the marked lines.

6   Starting with one of the longer lengths, centre the ribbon along the marked line and tack it into place. Using the appliqué foot and a narrow zigzag stitch, machine along both edges of the ribbon in the same direction.

7   Working away from the length of stitched ribbon, apply the other lengths to the right and to the left, always machining in the same direction.

8   Turn the work and complete the trellis effect with a second series of ribbons, crossing the first.

BINDING AND FINISHING

9   Attach the bias strip to the top edges, but do not fold over and complete yet.

10   Fold the bag in half crosswise and stitch up the side seams, including the binding. Neaten the seam with zigzag stitches. Fold over the binding and hem it into place.

11   To shape the base, turn the bag inside out, and stitch across the base at right angles to the side seams 1½in (4cm) from the bottom (see below).

12   Insert the zip by hand, stitching along the edge of the binding. Knot a short length of ribbon to the zip pull.

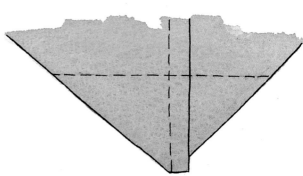

Shape the base of the bag

VARIATIONS

This method of combining ribbon appliqué with quilting can be used for all sorts of items, such as cushions, quilts, bags and garments.

You can vary the width and type of ribbon for different effects and combine it with other fabrics, such as velvet ribbon with satin, or woollen braid with tweed.

Printed ribbons with nursery motifs make pretty articles for children's rooms.

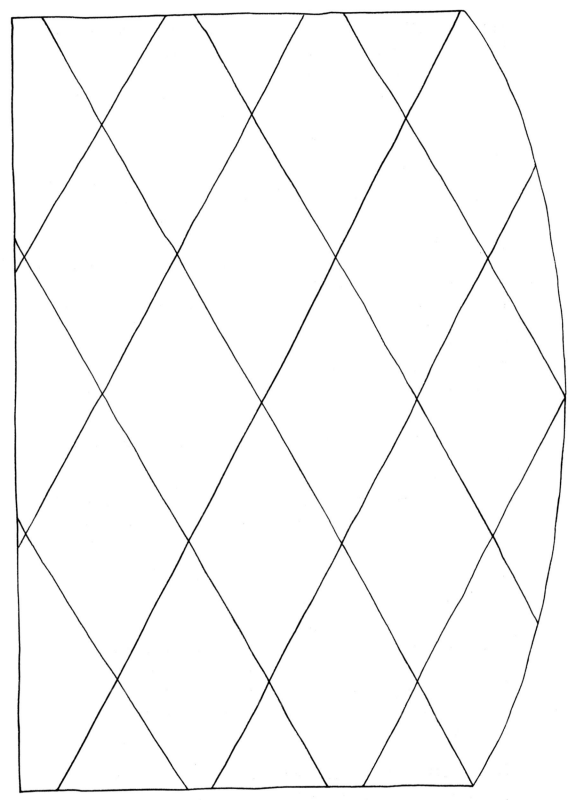

Template
Enlarge by 137%

BEADED
EVENING BAG

Large enough to hold everything necessary for that special

evening occasion, this silk evening bag combines couched

quilting in a pretty variegated thread and bugle beads. Make

it to match or contrast with your favourite outfit and

complete it with a handmade cord.

MATERIALS AND EQUIPMENT

Green silk, 2 pieces 18 x 6in (45 x 15cm)

Green silk, 6 x 1½in (15 x 4cm) straight strip for binding

Fine cotton backing fabric, 14 x 18in (35 x 45cm)

2oz wadding or domette, 18 x 6in (45 x 15cm)

Variegated embroidery yarn

Turquoise bugle beads

Green sewing cotton

Embroidery needle

Beading needle

12in (30cm) circular embroidery frame

Dressmaker's carbon paper and spent ballpoint pen

Tracing paper and pencil

Press stud for fastening

Sewing machine

Basic sewing equipment

PREPARATION

1   Use the template opposite and add a seam allowance (see opposite).

2   Enlarge the design template by 142% (see below) and transfer it to a piece of green fabric using dressmaker's carbon paper (see page 14).

3   Tack the fabric in the centre of the backing fabric with the wadding between, as for wadded quilting (see page 21) and mount it in the frame.

Design template
Enlarge by 142%

QUILTING

4   Using green sewing cotton, couch quilt the variegated embroidery thread along all the marked lines. On completion take all the ends through to the reverse side.

5   Stitch the bugle beads on the dotted lines traced on the fabric.

MAKING UP

6   Trim the backing fabric to the same size as the quilted silk and cut the lining to the same size.

7   With right sides together, pin, tack and machine stitch the lining to the quilted piece, leaving the straight end open, through which to turn the work.

8   Trim the backing and wadding to the seam, snip the curves and trim the bulk from the corners. Turn through to the right side and press the seam very lightly.

9   Bind the open edge (see page 29) with the strip of green silk, folding in both ends to neaten.

10   Fold the bag along the fold line and oversew the side seams together.

11   Make a twisted cord (see page 30) using six lengths of variegated thread, each 150in (375cm) long. Oversew the cord in place along the side seams, tucking in the ends between the front and back.

12 Stitch the press stud in place on the flap and front of the purse (see opposite).

VARIATIONS

This design can be adapted for Italian quilting along the double wavy lines. Use leftover fabric from a dressmaking project to make a matching bag.

Oversew cord around edge

Bind top edge

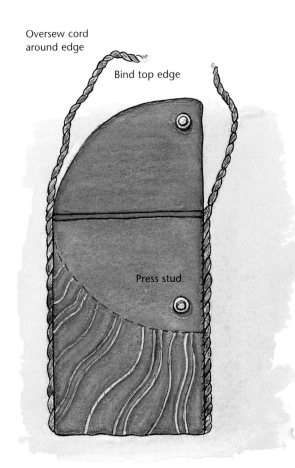

Press stud

Template

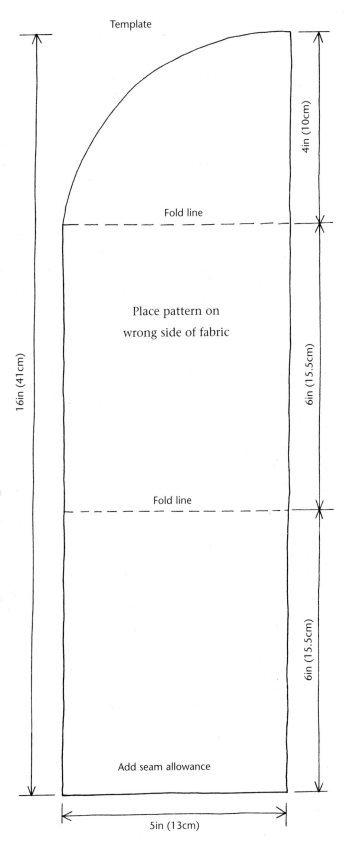

4in (10cm)

Fold line

Place pattern on wrong side of fabric

6in (15.5cm)

Fold line

16in (41cm)

6in (15.5cm)

Add seam allowance

5in (13cm)

ORGANZA EVENING SCARF

This diaphanous evening scarf will take you on all your evening dates. Use it to dress up a plain outfit or make one to match your favourite blouse or suit. Some types of transparent fabric will give slightly different effects as they may be more opaque or have different draping qualities.

MATERIALS AND EQUIPMENT

Pale blue nylon or silk organza, 2 pieces each 60 x 12in (153 x 30cm)

Cartridge paper, 11½ x 11½in (29 x 29cm), pencil and black felt-tip pen

Cotton or silk fabric in pink, yellow and blue, 4 x 4in (10 x 10cm) squares

Paper-backed fusible web, 8 x 8in (20 x 20cm) square

25–30 assorted sequin shapes, leaves, stars, hearts and flowers

Silver machine embroidery thread

Pale blue sewing cotton

Fabric marker

Masking tape

PVA adhesive and small brush

Sewing machine

Basic sewing equipment

DESIGN

1   On the cartridge paper, draw a wavy line diagonally from the bottom left-hand corner to the top right corner. Draw four more wavy lines approximately 1½in (4cm) apart across the corner, parallel with the first.

2   Draw a second series of nine wavy lines intersecting the first from bottom right to top left, finishing at the first line drawn.

3   When you are satisfied with your design, mark the lines with a black felt-tip pen. Mark alternate sections to indicate the areas to be decorated.

PREPARATION

4   Position the end of one piece of organza over the design and tape both the fabric and the paper securely to your work surface with masking tape. Trace the design using your chosen marker.

5   Iron the fusible web to the wrong side of the pink, yellow and blue squares of fabric and cut them into approximately forty small geometric shapes – squares, triangles and diamonds.

6   Peel off the backing paper from the backs of the small shapes and arrange them in the appropriate sections on the organza. Using a cool iron, press the snippets to adhere them to the organza.

7   Using a very small dab of PVA adhesive, glue one or two sequin shapes in each section.

MAKING UP

8   Pin and tack the second length of organza to the underside of the length you have decorated.

9   Machine stitch round the perimeter, with a ½in (1cm) seam allowance, leaving a small gap at the side, through which to turn the work. Trim the seam to ¼in (5mm).

10   Turn the scarf through to the right side and slip stitch the gap. Lightly press the seam and finish with a running stitch ¼in (5mm) from the edge.

11   To complete the entrapping, machine stitch along the marked intersecting lines using a medium-width zigzag in silver metallic thread.

VARIATIONS

This technique can be used with any transparent fabric such as voile, muslin, chiffon or net.

Experiment with different types of entrapped items such as snippets of ribbon or lace, beads, seeds, decorated paper or felt.

Decorate a net curtain or blind for your bathroom, entrapping seeds or shells in pockets along the hem.

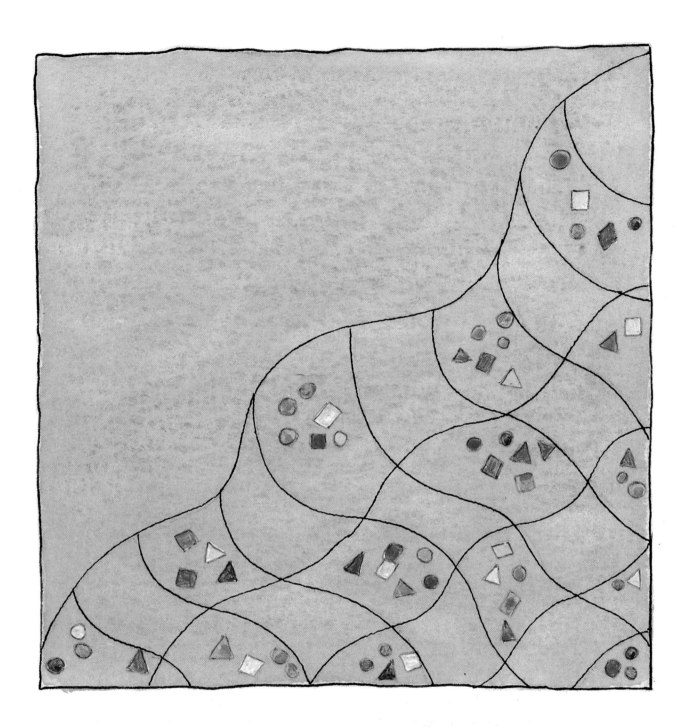

10 PRESENTS
FOR CHILDREN

Making quilted items for children is

fun. Waistcoats, jackets, hats and mitts

can all be padded and further

embellished with appliqué motifs. Cot

and bed quilts are an obvious creative

challenge, but smaller items such as

bags, mats and cushions can also

involve exciting and innovative designs.

WAISTCOAT WARMER

This snug reversible waistcoat will keep your toddler warm and happy. It will mix and match with everyday outfits or enhance a plain party dress. Choose a printed fabric with a bold design and a plain colour for the lining and machine quilt for a speedy result. This pattern will fit four- to six-year-olds, but the measurements can be easily adjusted by slightly altering the length and width.

MATERIALS AND EQUIPMENT

Printed cotton fabric, 20 x 45in (51 x 115cm)

2oz wadding, 20 x 35in (51 x 90cm)

Plain cotton fabric, 32 x 45in (81 x 115cm)

Matching sewing cotton

Squared drafting paper

Pencil and ruler

Sewing machine with appliqué foot

Basic sewing equipment

PREPARATION

1 Enlarge the template (see opposite) using squared drafting paper (see page 12).

2 Cut out the fabric, lining and wadding.

3 Pin and tack the wadding to the front and back pieces and stitch them together at the side and shoulder seams (see below). Trim excess wadding to the seams.

4 Stitch the lining fronts to the back at the side and shoulder seams.

5 Pin the lining into the waistcoat with the right sides together, matching the seams.

QUILTING

6 Tack up the three layers as for wadded quilting (see page 21).

7 Attach the appliqué foot to the sewing machine and machine quilt, following the design of the pattern. Start at the centre and work outwards, taking care not to pull or distort the shape.

BINDING

8 From the lining fabric, cut sufficient bias strips 1¾in (4.5cm) wide to make 22in (56cm) lengths for each armhole and 64in (162cm) for the outer edge.

Stitch side and shoulder seams

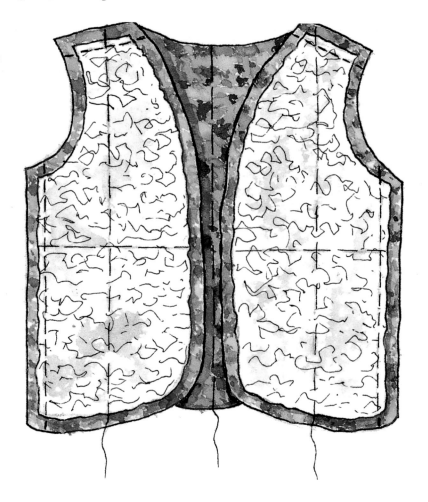

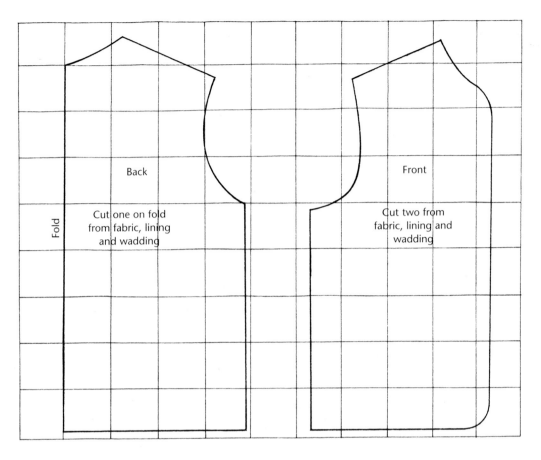

Back

Front

Fold

Cut one on fold
from fabric, lining
and wadding

Cut two from
fabric, lining and
wadding

9 Join the bias strips on the diagonal and attach binding round all the raw edges (see page 29).

VARIATIONS

This quilting method can be used for purchased pattern garments of different styles and sizes. For simple quilting, choose stripes or checks which you can quilt around.

For a decorative reversible effect, use a sewing cotton in the bobbin which contrasts with the lining fabric and bind with contrasting fabric.

HEIRLOOM COT QUILT

The birth of a new baby is a wonderful excuse for you to create an heirloom which can be cherished for years to come. Add the baby's name to the border and this will be a present to treasure, whether you are a parent, grandparent or simply a fond relative or friend.

MATERIALS AND EQUIPMENT

White polycotton or cotton, 2 pieces 39 x 51in (100 x 130cm)

2oz wadding, 39 x 51in (100 x 130cm)

Coloured tacking cotton

White tacking cotton

White quilting thread or sewing cotton

Fabric marker

Squared drafting paper and pencil

Tracing paper

Black felt-tip pen

Masking tape

Quilting frame, 12in or 14in (30cm or 35cm)

Basic sewing equipment

PREPARATION

1 Enlarge the design using squared drafting paper, 1 square = ½in (12mm). Complete the other three quarters by tracing.

2 Include the baby's name in the border and outline the design in black felt-tip pen.

3 For the direct tracing method (see page 13), position one piece of white fabric over the design and tape both securely to your work surface with masking tape. With the fabric marker, trace the design with a dotted line.

ASSEMBLING THE QUILT

4 Pin and tack the wadding to the underside of the top fabric on which you have marked the design, vertically, horizontally and diagonally and around the perimeter, using the coloured tacking cotton. Start and finish the tacking on the right side of the work.

5 Position the bottom fabric, right sides together on top of the top fabric. Pin, tack and machine stitch (or backstitch) around the perimeter, leaving a 12in (30cm) gap at the centre of one side, through which to turn the work. Trim off the excess wadding and turn the work through to the right side.

6 Press the seam lightly and slip stitch the gap. Tack a line of running stitches ½in (1cm) from the edge.

QUILTING

7 Pin and tack in a 4in (10cm) grid as for wadded quilting in white cotton. Then remove the coloured tacking threads.

8 If you are using a frame, mount up the central area first. Quilt with running stitches over the marked lines. On completion of the stitching within the confines of the frame, re-position it on an adjacent part of the design. Whether you are quilting with the work in your hand or in a frame, work from the centre towards the edge of the quilt, being careful not to distort the rectangular shape. It will be necessary to work the outer edge without the use of a frame. Remove traces of fabric marker if necessary.

9 Remove all tacking threads on completion. It is not advisable or necessary to iron the finished quilt, apart from a light pressing of the edge.

10 Don't forget to embroider your name and the date on the back of the quilt so that in years to come the quilt will become part of the family history.

VARIATIONS

If you prefer to quilt this project by machine, use the direct stitching method (see page 33).

This design can be adapted for an appliqué project or you can use fabric paints to fill in some of the motifs.

Design template
One square = ½in (12mm)

TOY BAG TIDY

Tidy up the nursery with this patchwork quilted and painted toy bag. Large enough for all those extra cuddly toys, bricks and games, it can be hung from a hook or the end of the cot and the thick padding prevents anything being damaged.

MATERIALS AND EQUIPMENT

Blue cotton fabric, 2 pieces 30 x 19½in (77 x 49cm)

4oz wadding, 2 pieces 30 x 19½in (77 x 49cm)

White cotton lining, 2 pieces 30 x 19½in (77 x 49cm)

Blue cotton fabric, 2 strips 19½ x 2in (49 x 5cm) for casing

5in (13cm) squares for patchwork, 5 pink, 3 yellow and 2 blue

Parallelograms for patchwork (see template), 4 white and 4 turquoise

Fabric pens in purple, green, dark green, red, blue, yellow and dark red

Masking tape

Tracing paper and black felt-tip pen

Fabric marker

Sewing cotton

Cord, 2 pieces 53in (135cm)

Bodkin or safety pin

Basic sewing equipment

PAINTING

1 Enlarge the motifs by 133% (see pages 132–3) and transfer them using a black felt-tip pen to the appropriate squares of fabric using the direct tracing method (see page 13).

2 Secure the first marked square to a work surface with masking tape and carefully fill in the design with the appropriately coloured fabric pen. Leave to dry and iron with a hot iron to fix the colour. Complete the rest of the squares.

PATCHWORK

3 Enlarge the template below by 133%. Cut four white and four turquoise parallelograms using the template.

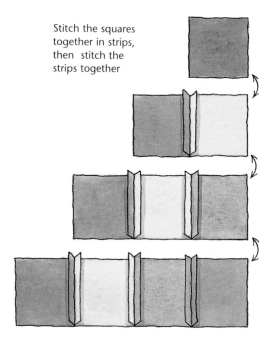

Stitch the squares together in strips, then stitch the strips together

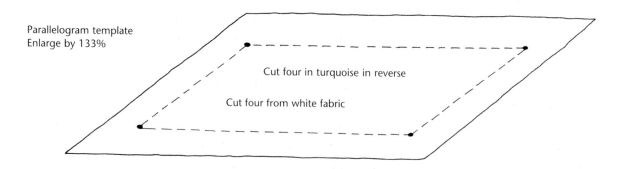

Parallelogram template
Enlarge by 133%

Cut four in turquoise in reverse

Cut four from white fabric

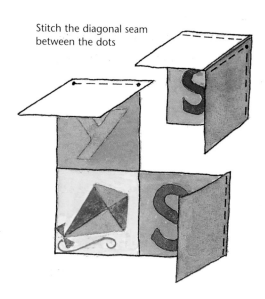

Stitch the diagonal seam between the dots

4 With right sides together, stitch the squares together to form four horizontal strips (see above). Then stitch these together, matching the seams, to form the building block design.

5 Add the parallelograms, alternating turquoise and white, (see left) along the right-hand diagonal edge, stitching only between the dots.

6   Stitch the diagonal seams of the parallelograms between the dots. Press and tack under the right-hand stepped diagonal edge.

APPLIQUÉ AND QUILTING

7   Tack the patchwork building blocks in place at the bottom edge of one piece of blue fabric.

8   Mark vertical lines on the blue fabric from the corners of the design and five vertical lines 4in (10cm) apart on the back fabric.

9   Tack the three layers of both front and back of the bag together for wadded quilting (see page 21).

10   Machine quilt along the marked lines on front and back, and round each building block.

MAKING UP

11   With right sides together, stitch the front to the back, leaving the top open. Neaten the seams and the top edge by overcasting by hand or machine.

12   Fold over the top edge to form a hem and slip stitch into place.

13   Join the two casing strips together, leaving a 1in (2.5cm) gap in the seam. Press a narrow hem along each long edge. Pin, tack and stitch the casing in place 4in (10cm) from the top edge.

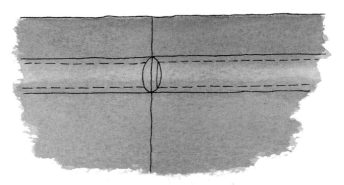

Join the casing strips leaving a gap in the seam

14   Thread the first cord through a bodkin or attach a safety pin, and insert through the casing, starting and finishing at the right-hand edge. Insert the second cord, starting and finishing at the left-hand edge. Tie the ends in a knot.

VARIATIONS

The building block design can be used for other nursery items, such as cot quilt, curtains or changing mat.

Make a similar bag for carrying nappies and changing equipment for trips away from home.

Enlarge by 133%

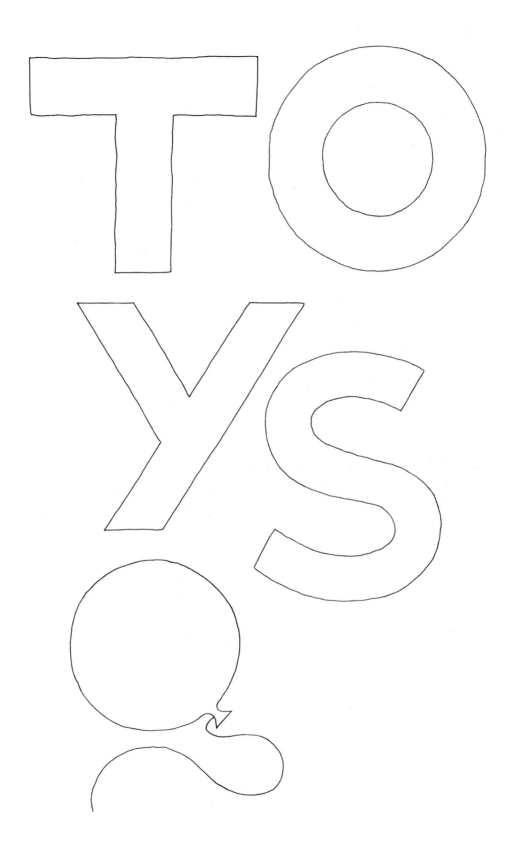

COLOURFUL PLAY MAT

Any baby will love to sit and play on this softly padded play mat. The three-dimensional geometric shapes are just the right size for a toddler to hold and learn to distinguish shapes and colour. Machine made and quilted with bright, colourful prints, this nursery accessory will give lasting amusement.

EQUIPMENT AND MATERIALS

Printed cotton, 35in (90cm) diameter circle for backing

Printed cotton, 3 strips 14 x 2in (35 x 5cm)

Printed cotton, 6in (15cm) diameter circle

Printed cotton, 12 border segments

Red, yellow and blue cotton segments, 23 x 15½in (59 x 39cm)

Red, yellow and blue cotton border segments, four of each colour

Red, yellow and blue cotton geometric patches

Red, yellow and blue cotton geometric pieces and wadding for three-dimensional shapes

Printed cotton geometric pieces for three-dimensional shapes

4oz wadding 35in (90cm) diameter circle

Iron-on interfacing for centre circle and geometric shapes

Red, yellow and blue sewing cotton

Red, yellow and blue fabric pens

6 Velcro 3in (8cm) strips

Squared drafting paper, ruler and pencil

Pair of compasses and protractor

Basic sewing equipment

PREPARATION

1   From the pattern, make a circular paper pattern 35in (90cm) in diameter for the backing fabric and wadding.

Play mat pattern 36in (90cm) diameter circle for backing and wadding

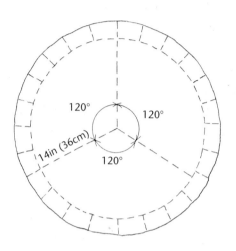

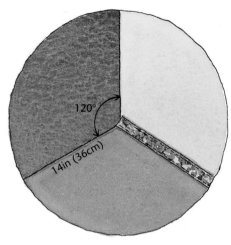

Stitch strips over seams

tack and stitch over the seams of the main pieces, working from the centre outwards along both edges (see above).

2   Using the protractor cut a smaller circle with a radius of 14in (35m) and divide it to give three segments each with an angle of 120 degrees. Add on the turnings.

3   Enlarge the fabric pieces for the segments and the border, strips and geometric shapes by 200% and cut them out (see pages 138–139).

4   Cut iron-on interfacing for centre circle and geometric shapes, omitting seam allowances (see pages 138–139).

PIECING THE TOP

5   With right sides together, stitch the three main pieces together, starting ½in (1cm) from the centre. Press the seams open.

6   Press a ¼in (5mm) hem along both long edges of the three fabric strips. Pin,

7   Iron the interfacing to the wrong side of the centre circle. Snip the curve and press and tack the fabric over the edge of the interfacing (see below). Pin, tack and top stitch to the centre of the play mat top.

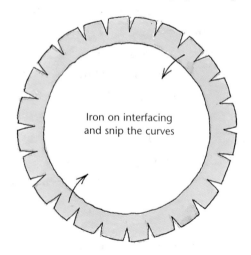

Iron on interfacing and snip the curves

8   For the border, join the segments, with right sides together, in three groups of eight: four red and four printed, four yellow and four printed, and four blue and four

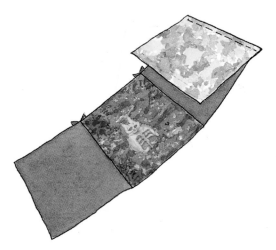

Join the border segments together

printed (see above. Then join these together to fit the outer edge of the play mat top.

9 Pin, tack and stitch the border to the play mat top, easing the curve and matching the change of colour to the centre of the applied strips.

GEOMETRIC SHAPES

10 Prepare the geometric shapes as for the centre circle. Snip the curves of the circle and trim excess fabric from the points on the diamond and triangle. Top stitch these in place on the play mat top.

MAKING UP

11 Pin the play mat top layer right side up on the wadding. Tack the pieces in grid formation to hold them together.

12 Pin and tack the backing fabric right sides together on top of the play mat top. Machine stitch round the perimeter, leaving a 6in (15cm) gap through which to turn the work.

13 Trim the wadding to the seam, turn through to the right side and stitch up the gap. Press the seam lightly.

14 Machine quilt around the inner edge of the border and round the centre circle.

THREE-DIMENSIONAL GEOMETRIC SHAPES

15 Using the fabric pens, colour the six Velcro strips: two each in red, yellow and blue. Allow to dry and press lightly to set the colour.

16 Stitch the fluffy pieces of Velcro to the correspondingly coloured geometric shapes on the play mat top and the rough pieces on the right side of the printed backs of the three-dimensional geometric shapes (see below).

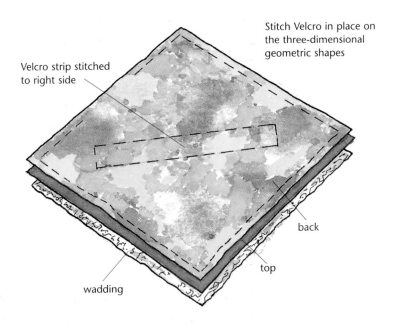

Stitch Velcro in place on the three-dimensional geometric shapes

Velcro strip stitched to right side

back

top

wadding

Enlarge all these templates by 200%

Border
Cut 12 in printed fabric
Cut 4 in each colour: red, yellow and blue
Cut 24 in interfacing
(no seam allowance)

17 Pin and tack corresponding coloured and printed pieces right sides together with wadding beneath. Stitch around the perimeter, leaving a gap through which to turn the work. Trim wadding to the seam, clip curves, and trim the excess fabric from points. Turn through to the right side, stuff with extra wadding if desired and stitch up the gap.

VARIATIONS

For a more ambitious design, replace the geometric shapes with animal motifs and small stuffed three-dimensional animals. Use this method for a quilted mat for other rooms in your home.

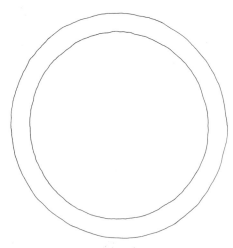

Circle
For three-dimensional shape
Cut one in printed fabric
Cut one in plain fabric

For centre circle
Cut one in plain fabric and one in interfacing
(no seam allowance)

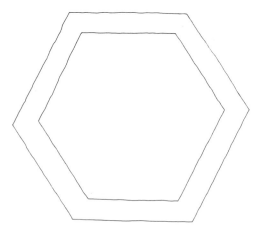

Hexagon
For geometric patch
Cut one in plain fabric
Cut one in interfacing
(no seam allowance)

For three-dimensional shape
Cut one in printed fabric
Cut one in plain fabric

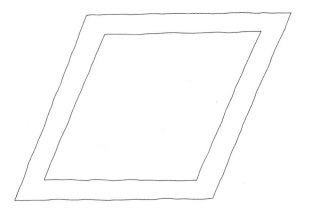

Parallelogram
For geometric patch
Cut one in plain fabric
Cut one in interfacing
(no seam allowance)

For three-dimensional shape
Cut one in printed fabric
Cut one in plain fabric

Square
For geometric patch
Cut one in plain fabric
Cut one in interfacing
(no seam allowance)

For three-dimensional shape
Cut one in printed fabric
Cut one in plain fabric

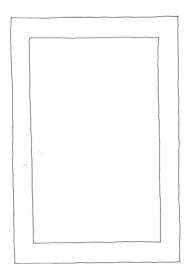

Rectangle
For geometric patch
Cut one in plain fabric
Cut one in interfacing
(no seam allowance)

For three-dimensional shape
Cut one in printed fabric
Cut one in plain fabric

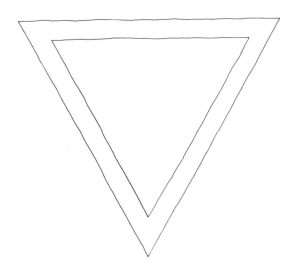

Triangle
For geometric patch
Cut one in plain fabric
Cut one in interfacing
(no seam allowance)

For three-dimensional shape
Cut one in printed fabric
Cut one in plain fabric

GALLERY

The craft of quilting has developed into an art which can extend the imagination of the maker and provide a vehicle for producing creative pictures, panels and garments. The wide range of quilting methods available lend themselves to being combined with other textile techniques such as patchwork, surface stitchery, appliqué or beading. Fabric paints and hand dyeing can bring additional individuality to the pieces, and contemporary designs and ideas are often used in tandem with traditional patterns.

ABOUT THE AUTHOR

Pauline Brown is an expert quilter and teacher of embroidery patchwork and textile crafts. She has already written several books on embroidery and appliqué.

Hannelore Braunsberg,
David's City,
30 x 53in (77 x 135cm)
Based on an etching by the
quilter's son. Machine pieced
with hand-applied silks and
cottons, with cotton wadding.
Photographed by
Suzanne Grundy.

Greta Fitchett,
Southwold Beach Huts – Moonlight,
80 x 80in (204 x 204cm)
Inspired by a holiday visit.
Machine pieced patchwork and
appliqué with free machine
embroidery and hand quilting
on hand-dyed calico and
commercially dyed cotton.

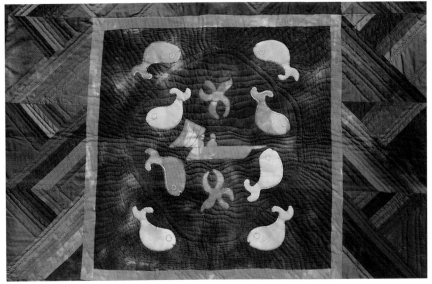

Greta Fitchett,
Ayasofia 2 Quilt,
11 x 15in (28 x 38cm)
Based on drawings made inside
the mosque in Istanbul. Machine
pieced patchwork, appliquéd felt
with machine embroidery and
quilting on hand-dyed calico, felt
and sheer viscose fabric.

Greta Fitchett,
Hearts and Tarts Tea Cosy,
15 x 11in (38 x 28cm)
Inspired by the quilter's own
baking. Machine quilting with
free machine embroidery on
polyester fabric.

Pauline Brown,
Sashiko Waistcoat
Design based on
patchwork templates
and geometric patterns.
Wool fabric with
quilting in pearl cotton.

Shirley Isaacs,
Indian Slippers
Handmade felt, lined
with silk and quilted
with metallic threads.
Decorated with shisha
motifs, beads and
decorative piping.

Elspeth Kemp,
Hannah's Quilt,
5 x 8ft (155 x 245cm)
Made to celebrate her
granddaughter's 21st
birthday. Hand quilted
throughout.
(Photographed by
Adshots, Hertford.)

Elspeth Kemp,
Gothic Lily Hanging,
5 x 8ft (155 x 245cm)
Inspired by medieval
designs with stylized
lilies, carnations and
pomegranates. Hand
stitched with handmade
tassels and cords.
(Photographed by
Adshots, Hertford.)

Pauline Brown,
Delphinium Temple,
16 x 20in (40 x 51cm)
Shadow Quilting with felt on tie-dyed background.
Suffolk puff flowers and free-standing leaves.

Margaret Mary Griffiths,
Spring,
17 x 17in (43 x 43cm)
A combination of silk appliqué and quilting worked in stab stitch and couching. The robin is enhanced with chain and feather stitch and the background with feather stitch.

Margaret Mary Griffiths,
Ravello,
18 x 19in (45 x 48cm)
The arcade of columns is trapunto quilted to raise it in relief from the painted silk background. The foreground wall is wadded with the pots in padded appliqué with flowers and foliage in a range of stitches.

INDEX

A

Art Nouveau photo frame 86–9

B

background designs 60
backing fabric 10
    tacking with backing fabric
        framed 21
backstitch 24, 25
beaded evening bag 110–13
beeswax 4
binding 29, 122–3
bolster cushion 64–7
borders 60
Braunsberg, Hannelore 141
Brown, Pauline 143, 146

C

cafetiere cosy 68–71
calico cushion 72–5
chain stitch 27
clematis trellis silk cushion 90–3
cords 30, 75
cosmetics bag 106–9
cot quilt 124–7
cotton 9
cotton wadding 10, 11
couch quilting 58, 110–13
couching 27

cushions 64–7, 72–5, 90–3
cutting equipment 3

D

decorative stitches 26–7, 97–8
design equipment 6–7
direct tracing 13, 15
Domette 10, 11
drawing, direct 15
drawing equipment 6
dressmaker's carbon paper 14

E

enlarging designs 12
entrapping 55–6, 114–17
evening bag 110–13
evening scarf 114–17

F

fabric markers 7, 130
fabrics 9–10
    preparing the fabric 12
fastening on 22
feather design 76–9
finishing off 22
Fitchett, Greta 141, 142
flat quilting 43
frames/framing 4, 18–20
French knots 98

fusible fleece 10, 11

G

geometric shapes 137–9
Griffiths, Margaret Mary 147

H

heirloom cot quilt 124–7
history of quilting 1–2

I

Isaacs, Shirley 143
Italian quilting 48–50, 52

K

Kantha quilting 45
Kemp, Elspeth 58, 144, 145

L

light box 15
long and short stitch 98

M

machine quilting 57–8, 90–3
man-made fibres 10
markers, fabric 7, 130

CRAFT TITLES AVAILABLE FROM
GMC PUBLICATIONS
BOOKS

CRAFTS

American Patchwork Designs in Needlepoint	*Melanie Tacon*
A Beginners' Guide to Rubber Stamping	*Brenda Hunt*
Celtic Cross Stitch Designs	*Carol Phillipson*
Celtic Knotwork Designs	*Sheila Sturrock*
Celtic Knotwork Handbook	*Sheila Sturrock*
Collage from Seeds, Leaves and Flowers	*Joan Carver*
Complete Pyrography	*Stephen Poole*
Contemporary Smocking	*Dorothea Hall*
Creating Knitwear Designs	*Pat Ashforth & Steve Plummer*
Creative Doughcraft	*Patricia Hughes*
Creative Embroidery Techniques	
Using Colour Through Gold	*Daphne J. Ashby & Jackie Woolsey*
The Creative Quilter: Techniques and Projects	*Pauline Brown*
Cross Stitch Kitchen Projects	*Janet Granger*
Cross Stitch on Colour	*Sheena Rogers*
Decorative Beaded Purses	*Enid Taylor*
Designing and Making Cards	*Glennis Gilruth*
Embroidery Tips & Hints	*Harold Hayes*
Glass Painting	*Emma Sedman*
An Introduction to Crewel Embroidery	*Mave Glenny*
Making and Using Working Drawings	
for Realistic Model Animals	*Basil F. Fordham*
Making Character Bears	*Valerie Tyler*
Making Greetings Cards for Beginners	*Pat Sutherland*
Making Hand-Sewn Boxes: Techniques and Projects	*Jackie Woolsey*
Making Knitwear Fit	*Pat Ashforth & Steve Plummer*
Natural Ideas for Christmas:	
Fantastic Decorations to Make	*Josie Cameron-Ashcroft & Carol Cox*
Needlepoint: A Foundation Course	*Sandra Hardy*
Pyrography Designs	*Norma Gregory*
Pyrography Handbook (Practical Crafts)	*Stephen Poole*
Ribbons and Roses	*Lee Lockheed*
Rubber Stamping with Other Crafts	*Lynne Garner*
Sponge Painting	*Ann Rooney*
Tassel Making for Beginners	*Enid Taylor*
Tatting Collage	*Lindsay Rogers*
Temari: A Traditional Japanese Embroidery Technique	*Margaret Ludlow*
Theatre Models in Paper and Card	*Robert Burgess*
Wool Embroidery and Design	*Lee Lockheed*

DOLLS' HOUSES AND MINIATURES

Architecture for Dolls' Houses	*Joyce Percival*
Beginners' Guide to the Dolls' House Hobby	*Jean Nisbett*
The Complete Dolls' House Book	*Jean Nisbett*
The Dolls' House 1/24 Scale: A Complete Introduction	*Jean Nisbett*
Dolls' House Accessories, Fixtures and Fittings	*Andrea Barham*
Dolls' House Bathrooms: Lots of Little Loos	*Patricia King*
Dolls' House Fireplaces and Stoves	*Patricia King*
Easy to Make Dolls' House Accessories	*Andrea Barham*
Heraldic Miniature Knights	*Peter Greenhill*
Make Your Own Dolls' House Furniture	*Maurice Harper*
Making Dolls' House Furniture	*Patricia King*
Making Georgian Dolls' Houses	*Derek Rowbottom*
Making Miniature Gardens	*Freida Gray*
Making Miniature Oriental Rugs & Carpets	*Meik & Ian McNaughton*
Making Period Dolls' House Accessories	*Andrea Barham*
Making Period Dolls' House Furniture	*Derek & Sheila Rowbottom*
Making Tudor Dolls' Houses	*Derek Rowbottom*
Making Unusual Miniatures	*Graham Spalding*
Making Victorian Dolls' House Furniture	*Patricia King*
Miniature Bobbin Lace	*Roz Snowden*
Miniature Embroidery for the Victorian Dolls' House	*Pamela Warner*
Miniature Embroidery for the Georgian Dolls' House	*Pamela Warner*
Miniature Needlepoint Carpets	*Janet Granger*
The Secrets of the Dolls' House Makers	*Jean Nisbett*

HOME & GARDEN

Bird Boxes and Feeders for the Garden	*Dave Mackenzie*
The Birdwatcher's Garden	*Hazel & Pamela Johnson*
Home Ownership: Buying and Maintaining	*Nicholas Snelling*
The Living Tropical Greenhouse:	
Creating a Haven for Butterflies	*John & Maureen Tampion*
Security for the Householder: Fitting Locks and Other Devices	*E. Phillips*

UPHOLSTERY

Seat Weaving (Practical Crafts)	*Ricky Holdstock*
The Upholsterer's Pocket Reference Book	*David James*
Upholstery: A Complete Course (Revised Edition)	*David James*
Upholstery Restoration	*David James*
Upholstery Techniques & Projects	*David James*

MAGAZINES

THE DOLLS' HOUSE MAGAZINE

CREATIVE CRAFTS FOR THE HOME

The above represents some of the books currently published or scheduled to be published.
All are available direct from the Publishers or through bookshops, newsagents and specialist retailers.
To place an order, or to obtain a complete catalogue, contact:

GMC Publications,
Castle Place, 166 High Street, Lewes, East Sussex BN7 1XU, United Kingdom
Tel: 01273 488005 Fax: 01273 478606

Orders by credit card are accepted